To my parents, Eldon and Gene Alig,
who were convinced that every life has meaning.

The Neighborhood

Tiptoeing into Poverty and Finding Hope

Leslie Alig Collins

authorHOUSE®

AuthorHouse™
1663 Liberty Drive
Bloomington, IN 47403
www.authorhouse.com
Phone: 1-800-839-8640

First published by AuthorHouse 9/15/2010

ISBN: 978-1-4520-6719-3 (sc)
ISBN: 978-1-4520-6718-6 (e)

Library of Congress Control Number: 2010911932

Printed in the United States of America

This book is printed on acid-free paper.

Contents

Foreword

This book deals heavily with suffering. As odd as it sounds, it is a story of one family's choice to suffer on purpose for the cause of Christ. There's no glory in suffering for show, as in suffering so that everyone's eyes will be on you. That's not what suffering on purpose is. Triumphant suffering puts everyone's eyes on the Savior.

Triumphant suffering seems like an oxymoron, but it's not. A public, pained countenance, for the sake of eliciting pity or attention is ... well, pitiful. On the other hand, mourning in true pain is normal. Faithful bravery in the face of hardship—because this is what you do, and because this is what Christ helps you to do—is honoring to Him. Overcoming distress and sadness after prayer and obedience is glorious. Can you see the difference? One situation is for the eyes of men; the other is for the heart of God.

***

One afternoon about six years ago I was in the basement of an inner-city Indianapolis church watching citizens of one of Indianapolis' meanest precincts line up for a free meal. I took up a spoon and dished chicken and noodles onto bendy paper plates held by people whose eyes were both proud and pleading. Most said thanks, while others just looked down. They apologetically came back for seconds. I thought they really appreciated people like me, from the northern Indianapolis suburbs, going to their rescue on a

Sunday afternoon, as though spooning food was a sacrifice of gargantuan proportions.

After we had wiped off the tables and the last of the people had left, I spoke with Jim and Debbie Strietelmeier who, with a band of committed relatives and friends, had for the past nine years lived and labored among the destitute population of East Tenth Street. The church/school/medical clinic they started there began as a small gathering, called Neighborhood Fellowship, in their living room. A book about the difference they had made in this dim place of hopelessness and crime had been swirling around in my head for about a year. I had already mentally written a number of chapter titles and scenarios.

I said, "Jim, I think I should write a book about Neighborhood Fellowship. Maybe we should pray about it."

His answer was so immediate as to surprise me: "I don't have to pray about it. It's a great idea. Just start."

With those marching orders, I set out to write a book, scared to death of the prospect of just starting. My decades in the newsroom and years of magazine writing were of no help in overcoming stark fear. And so, I circled the typewriter. I procrastinated. I cleaned house instead of starting what everyone came to call "The Book." But then I recalled the words of American aviator Eddie Rickenbacker: "Courage is doing what you're afraid to do. There can be no courage unless you're scared."

Instead of "praying about" writing "The Book"—and thus putting off the work of it—I prayed urgently and often for God to grant me the courage to do it. In ways I never imagined, God answered that prayer. The fact that He had to drag me downtown to actually *do the work* is the mark of His hand on this book. In the end, my urbane, suburbanite mindset was forever changed.

As the years went by after that day in the basement with the spoon and the pan and the poor, I often wondered why a year-long project had stretched into nearly a half a decade. God just wouldn't show me an ending. He would not let me rest. I lived in a state of agitation over it. I talked to myself, using all of the usual Christian clichés: "God's timing is not our timing." "God has something more." "Waiting on the Lord builds patience." "The Lord is waiting for you to …" What? What? What?

Finally, I had the whole thing done—or so I thought. But no, something just wasn't right. I talked to Jim; I harangued God.

No matter how hard I nagged and begged for direction and for the words to come, loose ends dangled like those chads on the Florida voting ballots of 2004. God's answer was to compel me to keep going back downtown for one more story, one more hour among the kids, one more day in the neighborhood, where it was so hard to go. I was drawn like a kid to a mud puddle. I just had to keep jumping in, no matter how messy it was. And after each plunge—pure joy!

Kids who eyed me with suspicion for a good year slowly gave me their ever-so-fragile friendship. Downtown, I didn't have to "be" anything but myself. Sometimes, I was naïve and annoying, but poor people have bigger things to worry about than whether I'm naïve. It was both difficult and freeing to truly learn about the attitudes and prejudices to which many people like me cling to as we pretend to adhere to biblical condemnation of such things. I let go of lofty ideas and took hold of simply doing the work.

"I'm not the founder of the school," Jim once wrote to me. "That honor belongs to Joy Elliot and Linda Jackson, my mother-in-law."

It would do well to insert here the progression of events

leading to the school. Jim and Debbie were founders of Neighborhood Fellowship, the church that parented and now houses the school. Jim continues to pastor the church, though he'd rather be in Africa.

Jim demurs when it comes to taking credit. The only time he points to himself is when there's work to be done. Now he'll say I'm making him sound like a saint. Well, he and his wife, Debbie, are saints, but not because they have a ministry to the poor. It's because they are followers of the Lord Jesus Christ and their faith is at the core of everything they do. They would describe themselves as average people doing the Lord's work.

Jim once told me, as I lamented over the never-ending book, "You can't write an ending to something that has no end." And so, I finally put a period at the end of the last sentence and got up, saying to myself, "It's done."

The book may be done, but the story is not. By the time you read here that a student drifted away to unknown places, he or she might be back in class. When you read that a junkie is a changed person because of God's work at Neighborhood Fellowship, do so knowing that addiction, like cancer, can go in and out of remission.

Just know that the last chapter of this book will be written in heaven.

Neighborhood Academy kids and aides line up during recess to watch activity in the gymnasium. From left are Kim, Kristy Alsmeyer Walsman, Johnny, Joel Walsman with Mimi Glaser on shoulders, John, an intern, and Jofus.

1

Meet Neighborhood Academy

As I step into the century-old church building, grit crunches under my Birkenstocks. I should have worn socks. I look down at the floor and feel sadness at the oldness of the cracked, black and gray diamond shapes that used to be decent linoleum. In their day, they were probably black and white. I trudge up the staircase holding the sticky wood banister while making a mental note to stop at the drug store for some hand sanitizer on the way home. The pharmacist will know the strongest brand. I tell myself that the railing was probably once polished to a high sheen. The first thing I remember thinking when I step into the lone classroom at Neighborhood Academy is: "Boy, they're going to need some bigger desks in here. Could somebody please give these people a leg up?"

***

Jim Streitelmeier, a pastor on the younger end of middle age, sits folded into a child-size chair. He and a teenager are hashing out the answer to a math story problem, seated at a table more suited to second-grader. Never mind. It's learning that's important in this Neighborhood Academy classroom.

Neighborhood. Sounds like a sunny cul-de-sac where happy kids play ball and ride bikes.

Academy. The word seems fitting for a private school in the suburbs where it's not uncommon for homes to have entire nightclubs in their basements and vast upper-floor suites for the seclusion and comfort of harried parents.

Neighborhood Academy is none of the above. It's smack dab in the middle of an area riddled with every known form of twenty-first-century urban pestilence.

When I started visiting Neighborhood Academy regularly in 2004, the entire school was one room on the second floor of a century-old church building that bore the scars of neglect. To get to the school room, I made my way down a cavernous hallway and past rooms scattered randomly with institutional tables, metal folding chairs and unmatched shelving. Here and there were sagging couches people had donated with the good intention of upgrading the church and school.

The academy status of this place comes from the heart of the school, not from a measure of its furnishings. Its students are salted away from the destruction and failure of inner-city public schools—not by distance, but by philosophy.

Going there wasn't easy in the beginning. I live a relatively comfortable life in the suburbs. People like me go to college, take our kids to Little League and soccer and are room mothers at school. We don't generally gravitate toward problematic situations if we don't have to. And so, making trips to the forlorn precinct of Neighborhood Fellowship Church and its tiny academy started out as a dismal task, especially on rainy days. I'm usually sad to begin with on rainy days. Driving south of the polite areas of town, I'd go from sad to depressed. Feeling shallow, I confessed this one day to Jim, who laughed out loud and said, "I don't blame you. I get depressed about it all the time. But Jesus Himself was a man of sorrows, acquainted with grief."

The trips downtown were to become the highlight of my week, and its children a source of great joy and marvelous revelation. I just didn't know it yet.

On the face of it, the neighborhood just east of Tenth and Rural streets on Indianapolis' near east side is a place where gloom is etched on the faces of unkempt men who wear linty woolen caps even in the summertime and who roam the streets aimlessly as though they've stayed too long—like grimy roadside snow that has long since worn out its welcome. The inhabitants of the place have largely become as run down as the buildings whose heyday splendor came and went in the first half of the twentieth century.

For the children who live in this landscape, Neighborhood Academy is a gift. There is no tuition and no exam to exclude anyone. For most, it provides eight hours a day of relief from relentless trouble. After all, how much trouble can a story problem be to a kid whose parents are likely at home smoking crack?

Neighborhood Academy operates from the premise that there is promise in every household, street and block.

Jim and Debbie Strietelmeier and their three children could have stayed in the suburbs back in the mid-1990s, when Jim worked at a gas station in the upper-crust suburb of Zionsville, Indiana, cheerfully pumping gas and otherwise serving the people he knew from his church. The same people would later serve with him in the inner city—sometimes humbly and sometimes not.

While he held the gas station job, Jim was an intern for Zionsville Fellowship, a church with roots in the 1970s bolt from conventional religiosity to the simplicity of the early church. Those involved in this movement called it a revival

3

or a renewal. His internship, combined with their childhood experience, graduation from Moody Bible Institute in Chicago, and missionary service in Africa, were the training grounds that prepared the Strietelmeiers to work in the trenches of trouble. They long to return to Africa, but their dark continent, for now, is urban Indianapolis.

The Bible was the source of their decision to take their children and move south to the city. They take seriously the passages that predict suffering for committed Christians. Jim points to one verse in particular: "For it has been granted to you on behalf of Christ not only to believe on him, but also to suffer for him …" (Philippians 1:29)

The Strietelmeiers couldn't just talk about suffering for the cause of Christ. Talk's cheap. They chose to live out the words. For them, that meant not waiting around for distress to come their way, but to seek it out. To choose suffering. Their deliberate walk into the storm landed them on east Tenth Street, where nothing much grows in the dirt that surrounds buildings and weedy parking lots. In their new neighborhood, they found one out of every five existing homes vacant, boarded up, or in major disrepair.

From this rude setting sprang Neighborhood Academy. Now, more than a decade later, love blooms there, packaged in an old building's worn walls. The Strietelmeiers and the band of fellow laborers have nurtured and grown a hub of kindness, warmth, and spiritual guidance in the midst of desolation.

Over the years, it became easier to go there, even on those down-in-the-dumps rainy days. I no longer trudge down there, feeling like an impostor because I drummed up a cheerful face while feeling a certain sadness over the sheer weight of poverty and trouble. After all, bottomless pits of trouble take getting used to. As time passed, I never failed to find God's mercy inside those doors. I would put on the face, do the work, and leave blessed. I found undeserved mercy, every time. Joy found me in the midst of relentless suffering.

***

The story problem Jim and the girl named Kim—a round-faced girl with brownish-blonde hair slicked back into a ponytail—were working on that day was about determining the interest rate on cash—foreign territory for the mystified teen, who sat there looking bored. Chances are it will remain foreign, even as she grows up. But Jim likes taking chances.

And so, Jim explains the story problem to Kim: "You're going to find that you have to multiply the days. There are 365 days in a year. This is what bankers do."

A light bulb switches on in her head, and Kim brightens at this explanation, going on in earnest to figure out the answer.

She does not know if she'll graduate from high school this year, but she's philosophical. A handwritten sign on crookedly torn paper hanging over her school desk reads, "You may be disappointed if you fail, but you're doomed if you don't try."

Little do the teacher and the student know that in a few short weeks Kim's father will be dead of a drug overdose and that Jim will be presiding over the funeral. Kim will be dealing with a lesson too horrific and too big for her seventeen years—a tutorial of suffering that will impact her life more deeply than a lesson on investments.

Jim is not trying to help her escape the neighborhood. He is trying to help her cope with what is, trying to get her to see there's a world beyond crumbling sidewalks, barred store windows, and empty-eyed prostitutes who hawk their bodies across the street from the school.

Prostitution is not always across the street. I remember the day I went looking for Jim outside, thinking I might find him in the church van, parked out front. As I walked toward the van, I saw a woman pulling up her jeans as a man sat watching on a wall shoring up a garden of weeds.

Now, by this time I should have been seasoned to this sort of thing, having watched Jim on numerous occasions shoo prostitutes and Johns from the building. But hearts pound when evil looms, and my heart was thundering.

Should I turn and walk away? Should I cross the street? Who knew what kind of lunacy lurked over there? Why, oh why, did I ever leave the safety of the church?

I decided that shock and horror weren't the way to go, so I just went about my business and acted nonchalant. I averted my eyes, wishing I was anywhere but there.

Down the street, Jim was not in the van. I had to walk back past the offending people—*alone.* I felt anything but nonchalant or polite. I felt the awful loneliness of being in the wrong place.

The woman was still yanking at her skin-tight jeans. I remembered some advice Jim had given me about the dangers of exhibiting suburban politeness on the street: "That kind of politeness gets no respect."

Not that I wanted to be respected by these two. I just didn't want to be a victim, and I for sure didn't want to seem as though all of this was okay with me. Fighting the urge to mold my face into a polite, inane smile, I looked straight ahead, blankly. As I walked by, the man snickered and said, "Everything's okay here."

"I'm not so sure about that," I blurted, out of nowhere and kept on walking. I was glad I had said it.

I thought of the children inside the building, and part of me wanted to turn and strangle these people who would add their sordid corruption to the troubles already wrought upon the children's lives. Forgive me, Lord, for breaking the commandment about murder.

Later, Jim scolded me for walking alone on the sidewalk, saying that I should have immediately gone into the building to find him. I reminded Jim he wasn't in the building, which was why I was out on the street in the first place. He laughed and asked if I had taken notes. Jim always wanted to know if I was taking notes for "The Book."

But hey, spring is here, so who can help being outside? I ask Jim if he is relieved to have some time off—spring break, you know. He just laughs out loud. "The insanity doesn't end at spring break. It just moves over here to our house and takes up residence."

***

Jim Strietelmeier tutors the kids but also acts as janitor, bus driver and security guard. He was instrumental in the founding of Neighborhood Academy, along with a host of quiet Barnabas-types who have faithfully backed the effort since 1996 after Debbie's mother, Linda Jackson, and friend Joy Elliott came up with the idea for the school.

Debbie's father, Phil Jackson, now a widower, is the senior pastor at the church and stoic school watchman. During one of my visits in 2006, I find Phil sitting patiently in the classroom watching for opportunities to be useful as person-in-charge Jessie Glaser plods through a mountain of paperwork at a huge, old wooden office desk. Phil offers grandfatherly help to kids struggling with their lessons. To maintain order, he has only to quietly speak the name of the one who's shooting a rubber band or jostling other students.

As Phil monitors the dozen or so kids, he glances wistfully out the new windows installed that week, donated by a local window company. The sashes and panes gleam against the old, dark building. The early spring sun blazes into the classroom that day without the filter of ancient dust and grime that had, for decades, cast a dank pall over the rooms of the church building. Keeping order is easier in a decent atmosphere.

In the upstairs hallway leading to Neighborhood Academy, a faded plastic flower bouquet blooms in a defunct porcelain drinking fountain attached to the wall. Big, bright rooms that have seen the hand of help radiate from the darkened corridor where stacks of long tables and lengths of wood stand waiting for a purpose. The clutter hides some of the peeling plaster walls. Someone years ago threw down a long carpet remnant but seemingly never bothered with it again. It covers the aged brown linoleum that is splitting in chunks from the wooden floor beneath. It's no use sweeping up every day. Sweeping is the least of their worries down here.

In stark contrast, new ductwork gleams overhead, snaking along into the bright classroom like an arrow pointing to a place of hope: "Follow me. Here's a happy place."

Jim Strietelmeier helps a student with computer work at Neighborhood Academy in 2006.

2

Suffering on Purpose

With a perpetually optimistic focus centered on his destiny of serving the poor, Jim Strietelmeier usually looks as though he got dressed in a hurry. It's not that he's a slob, but he has neither the time nor desire to preen in front of a mirror. His life teems with pressing issues, and one of them isn't his shirt—or his beard, which is sometimes trimmed, sometimes not. Periodically, he's on a diet. All of the time, he's available—except electronically.

"Don't bother sending me e-mails because I probably won't read them," he cheerfully advised everyone shortly after someone invented e-mail. The advice remains today. E-mails are too much trouble, but going down to the county jail with a crying neighbor who knocks at his door at midnight to say her husband had been arrested is not.

He is widely known for losing his cell phone and probably won't remember that you had penned in an appointment with him at a certain hour. Bother him anytime in person, though, and he'll greet you with a smile and sit down for a long talk. You'll never know you just interrupted him. He's about the business of just being there.

Debbie is about caretaking—for her own four children and two adopted ones; for the school, and seeing to it that lunch is ready, and for presiding over giant meal tables in their home. She is organized and usually knows where the cell phone is. She keeps her long, brown hair neatly pulled back into a ponytail.

The Strietelmeiers have felt the sting of learning that, to some observers, their work is morose entertainment, considering the relentless hardship of the people who live along East Tenth Street. They've been prodded and examined by reporters, the intrusions into their lives sometimes resulting in articles that brought dismay to the faces of Neighborhood Fellowship people who never before saw themselves as misfits. Their world, after all, had always seemed predictably ordinary to them. Nobody down here spends their money at Abercrombie & Fitch or Crate & Barrel. Everybody is used to hearing gunshots and witnessing mayhem. They just duck and dodge and go on about their business, watching their back. Most people's homesteads are in sorry need of paint and topsoil. So what?

When they have a few bucks for gas, people down here might mow the patches of crabgrass and chickweed they call a lawn—and that's only if they managed to get their hands on some sputtering piece of machinery that was once a real lawn mower. Otherwise, they consider the weeds part of the landscaping.

After the news reporters come and go, the Strietlemeiers and the people they shepherd often read printed versions of themselves that are unfamiliar, depending on the writer. The curious but unconcerned writers simply use the people's distress to hook and entertain readers. This type of mainstream journalist doesn't go on to tell about the value of suffering that Jim and Debbie painstakingly outline in every interview. Their declarations of joy in the midst of sorrow are generally dismissed as mere sidelines—if included at all.

What do they mean by "the value of suffering"? In the eyes of the world at large, there is no value in having no transportation to work. The world sees no glory in dealing daily with drugs and crime—or in being robbed several times a year, or in fearing for your life because you unwittingly violated some vague, hallowed gang rule.

"We have a theology of suffering," Jim explained to me one day in the hallway outside the academy classroom. "We don't look around for how we can suffer more. We could put our hand in the fire and do that. We just use the suffering we already have. God teaches, and we are the illustration. The godly result is the value of it."

So here they are, transplanted from the suburbs into what Indianapolis Police Maj. Lloyd Crow described to me in 2007 as the poorest, meanest area of the city. The murder here of an entire family was so notorious that *The New York Post* on August 6, 2006, used it as a catalyst for a major article detailing downtown Indianapolis's rising crime rate. The piece ended with this chilling account: "The recent violence follows the June 1 slayings of seven people in an east side home, the city's worst mass killing in 25 years."

I wasn't all that surprised to learn that the "east side home" mentioned in the article was within two blocks of the Strietelmeier home on Beville Street, which is within walking distance of the church. Ten years earlier, Jim and Debbie had moved their own family into this mess of a place to live out their calling to become one with the people they serve. To suffer on purpose.

They moved downtown to gain higher ground with the lowly and destitute, to partake in their vision of redemption for thieves, murderers, gang members, and the everyday people who became their new neighbors. There was no other way but to become poor themselves.

For all of their determination, there's no denying the stress of it all. For sanity's sake, after several years Jim started taking Fridays off from church and school duties, "to hide from the madness." The Friday madness escape has gotten shorter over the years. It's now down to Friday evening family time, if no one needs anything.

Debbie once wrote, "We don't do this because it is fulfilling. It is hard work and sometimes unpleasant. Fulfillment comes from obedience to God. Joy comes from the Spirit and living out the beatitudes."

Others came downtown with the Strietelmeiers: Debbie's parents, Phil and Linda Jackson; Mike and Cindi Hale; and Barry and Jessie Glaser. Later, others moved to the area—married couples, young interns—all hoping their move would fill the gaping hole left by urban natural selection—the able and savvy who were born to poverty managed to make good and then fled.

***

Jim's road to Neighborhood Fellowship rambles purposefully through a middle-class childhood, followed by college at Moody Bible Institute and a missionary stint in Africa with Debbie.

Jim's life story is a picture of the culture clash we see in every city in America. His father disowned Jim after a confrontation over his father's intention to divorce his mother. Jim's father, who claimed to be a Christian, had the suburban mindset of power, wealth and comfort. His mother, raised in a poorer culture, thrived on relationships. That was the difference between them that could not be bridged. As Jim worked to forgive his father in all of this, he learned that the ability to forgive builds a strong bridge between cultures.

He remembers childhood summers during the 1970s driving to and working on his grandmother's Indiana farm but living in the old-moneyed, upper-crust Meridian Kessler section of greater Broad Ripple, a middle-class neighborhood on the north side. In those days, bungalow homes and small brick cottages on streets with names like Rural, Primrose and Broadway were apt renderings of the everyday folk who populated Broad Ripple. In the 1950s, the anchor stores in this neighborhood were Hedlund's Hardware and the Kroger grocery store. On Saturdays, kids—including me— amused themselves at the Vogue Theater, which for a quarter admission showed feature movies preceded by educational film reels and *Looney Tunes* cartoons. Hedlund's is still there, but the Vogue became a nightclub in 1977.

Meridian Kessler is a step up from Broad Ripple, with one- and two-story early 1900s-era brick homes laden with leaded-glass windows, gables, turrets and slate roofing.

In the late 1970s, the chamber of commerce put up signs calling Broad Ripple a "village," in hopes of drawing customers and new businesses to the flagging 1960s headshops and cluttered stores along College Avenue. Coffee shops, cozy eateries and boutiques moved in as did the hip, the young and the trendy, who spruced up the bungalows and turreted homes. A greenway trail was installed, called The Monon, named for a rail line whose abandoned bed became the trail. A Starbucks came to town, and all was well in Broad Ripple.

But in Jim's day, it was a nice, blue/white-collar neighborhood, where kids went to Indianapolis Public School No. 84 and on to Broad Ripple High School.

His family attended church at Wheeler Mission downtown in the 200 block of North Delaware Street. The

Mission is a Christian haven for the homeless and destitute. But in those early days, it was the precursor to Jim's affinity for the downtrodden.

As teens attending Wheeler, Jim and his pal, Barry Glaser, often walked past prostitutes and pimps on their way along dirty side streets to buy snacks for too much money in too-fluorescent convenience stores. Barry now labors daily as Neighborhood Academy's administrator. His wife, Jessie, likewise grew up attending Wheeler and works at the school checking worksheets, teaching, keeping order, being motherly. She's so motherly, in fact, that as of this writing, she has nine children at home, including three young boys they adopted in 2008. Their oldest, Gabby, is studying at Moody Bible Institute in Chicago.

Barry and Jim, both 43 as of fall 2009, have been friends since they were 14. In those early days of their friendship, they'd meet at Wheeler and hang around downtown or at Burger Chef, where they worked serving fast food. Barry sometimes would go with Jim out to Jim's grandparents' farm where, it's said, Barry once accidentally shot Jim in the head with a BB gun—but no scars were borne, and the two grew to manhood with a common desire to return to the old neighborhood.

The summer after Jim's 17th birthday, he headed for Camp Hunt in Bloomington, about 50 miles south of Indianapolis. The camp is Wheeler Mission's summer outreach to poor children. Jim was a counselor that summer, when he met 15-year-old Debbie Jackson, daughter of Phil and Linda.

***

The eleventh anniversary of Neighborhood Fellowship was October 29, 2007. To be honest, nobody knew whether the church ministry would last for even a year back in 1996 when the Strietlemeiers moved downtown. They had spent 1990–91 in Durbin, South Africa, living in a half-double near the Gandhi settlement. Abigail was conceived in Durbin, where they ministered to Hindus. To this day, they want to return.

"I'd like to get there before I'm 50," Jim said.

It was not to be—at least, not yet. Could it be that God was leading them back into a downtown Indianapolis setting similar to where Jim grew up? Africa is worlds away. Indianapolis was 11.6 miles from Zionsville. And so, Tenth and Rural would become their Africa.

Armed with the blessings of Zionsville Fellowship and Eagle Creek Fellowship churches and the prayers of both far-north suburban congregations, Jim and Debbie packed up their two kids and their belongings and set out for the inner city. The weedy, run-down double they moved into on Beville was near a couple of crack houses. With help from the two Northside churches, Jim and Debbie bought the structure, aiming to make it a single-family home that would accommodate a good number of people, since Neighborhood Fellowship would start out as a house church.

Along with Jim and Debbie came their children, Abigail, then 5, and Elizabeth, almost 3. Moses would follow, then Joseph. Phil and Linda Jackson moved in with them.

Eager people packing tools, time and expertise came from the Zionsville and Eagle Creek churches to begin renovating the house. There were walls to take out, drywall to put in, floors to refinish, ceilings to repair and spackle and paint to slap on.

The household grew.

"As we were starting to knock out the walls, we knew my mother was coming," Jim said. "Then my grandmother fell, and we knew she was coming here, too. Her name was Ottie Pearl Smith."

It became even more evident that their mission would require all of the faith and courage they could muster. Jim tells of gunfights and drug wars on his street. He and Debbie worried about the safety of their own two little girls. They had good cause.

One day that first summer, 3-year-old Elizabeth and her little friend were playing outside on the swing set. In the broad daylight, when all seemed as well as could be expected, Debbie heard the distinct crack of a gunshot. She raced for the kitchen and saw the girls coming inside, wide-eyed and scared.

"As soon as we heard the bullet, we came inside the house, Mommy," Elizabeth said, earnestly.

Heart pounding, Debbie maintained a stoic front. "Good," she said to the girls. "You made the right decision."

Then she went into the other room and cried.

***

Though they were prepared to enter this netherworld culture that the majority of us would never choose, having stray bullets whizzing across their backyard came as a shock. Consider their backgrounds.

Jim's father, James Henry Strietelmeier, came from the gilded side of the family. James married Mary Smith, the daughter of Ottie Pearl Smith and her sharecropper husband. Mary's side of the family was made up of country folk who were obliviously content with their no-frills lifestyle. Still, Jim told me that Mary smarted at the remembrance of those times in the mid-1960s when people called her family "Appalachian white."

They lived with James Henry's mother in her nice house in the Meridian Kessler area.

Jim candidly looks at his heritage this way: "I was

half Appalachian white and half Meridian Kessler. That's why I could fit between the two cultures of suburbs and the inner city. I knew what they both were. The fact that I'm both is useful to our ministry. It's the lynchpin in our relationships."

But the diversity of cultures made for conflict between James Henry and Mary. He liked the "finer things in life," while she was happily unpretentious.

James Henry's finer things in life came from Grandma, who demanded the allegiance of her son and did not hide her opinion that his wife was a bumpkin. Year by year, the wedge between James and Mary grew.

"It was like the gash in rock that started the Colorado River and then became the Grand Canyon," Jim said.

James filed for divorce when Jim was 30. Jim advised his father that, for a person claiming to be a Christian, this was just not right. James resented Jim's counsel, disowned his son and went off to live his own life. At James's insistence, the two haven't spoken in more than 12 years, though his father still lives in the same Meridian Kessler house, just two blocks from another church Jim and Debbie help care for in Broad Ripple called Olive Branch.

When Jim talks about this most painful part of his life, he interjects humor, bringing to mind the old saying, "If I don't laugh, I'll cry."

Debbie only knew the beauty of Western American countrysides growing up as a missionary kid. Her parents were affiliated with the Rural Home Missionary Association. She spent half her growing-up years as a minority in rural, Hispanic Las Vegas, New Mexico. The family then moved to scenic Sierraville, California. She didn't know what to expect in 1996 as she and Jim plunged into their new life at Tenth and Rural.

"Mountains and streams. That was all I knew, so I was

afraid for the kids' safety and their relationships. I didn't want to frighten them," she said. "When we moved here, we made clear rules about staying in the yard and not talking to people walking down the street. I remember being with them most of the time when they played outside."

She says they wonder to this day, sometimes, whether they've done the right thing. She weighs in on the intellectual and emotional tug of war:

"When you're following God, and you're in the midst of it, you wonder a little bit, is this crazy thing we're doing really what He wants? Then you look at Scripture, and that is what sustains you. When you are doing what's in God's word to do—caring for the poor—you know intellectually you are doing the right thing. But on an emotional level, you still have those feelings of doubt. God is interested in obedience."

Flashes of memory remind Debbie that God shows her His will through everyday life—such as the time Abigail and Elizabeth came down the stairs after their baths. By the time they reached the bottom step, they were dirty again, and Debbie's heart sank. After all, Abby was two years old when she got really dirty for the first time. Here were her two little girls, baby-fresh clean moments ago, now looking like kids leading hard-scrabble inner-city lives.

But it was an eye-opening moment for Debbie.

"I thought of how I see all of these dirty little kids in the 'hood and now I know why. There's no grass. They're outside. Old houses are dusty. I began to think that maybe I didn't understand as much as I thought I did about why people in the city live the way they do. God was telling me that these experiences would help me understand more about the lives of the people I was living with," she said.

Even their missionary work in Africa and Chicago had

not prepared the Strietelmeiers for the cruder side of life in urban Indianapolis.

Now, they counted more than ever on the undergirding prayers and encouragement from the Zionsville and Eagle Creek churches. People would try to give food, clothing, watches, and money to Jim, but he always gave the stuff and the money away. If you took a Thanksgiving turkey down because you thought the Strietelmeiers could use a good meal, Jim would thank you and say he knew just the person who needed this.

"We are not just ministering to the poor," Jim said. "We *are* the poor."

***

The family's refusal to live higher off the hog than their neighbors spoke volumes. In time, the transplanted, four-generation household became one with the neighborhood.

Jim went door to door and invited people he met on the street to come worship at their home alongside handful of Northside supporters. In the Strietelmeiers' newly expanded living room, where a long, antique pew served as a couch, 21 people met for church that first Sunday, October 29, 1996. Chairs were dragged in from the dining room. Phil and Jim accompanied the singing at the piano and on the guitar.

One thing the Strietelmeiers learned in Africa served them well here: don't bring your culture into the neighborhood. They found early on that an urban setting is no place for early-morning church services. People without transportation need to be rounded up. People who are jobless don't tend to get up early. The employed are likely working the least-desirable graveyard shift, so they're asleep until 2:00 or 3:00 PM.

Late afternoons proved best for church services, and providing food followed the New Testament example of a home church. Debbie and Jessie cooked furiously in the kitchen to feed those who showed up. The combination of church and a meal worked. The custom continues today, with added bonuses from friends. In one instance, a man from Zionsville regularly sends piles of specialty breads for the Sunday lunches. More often than not, though, the bread goes out the door to hungry people who knock at the church doors on weekdays. Whenever the food pantry gets low, the northern churches put squibs in their bulletins and the shelves fill up again.

The now-crumbling Rivoli Theatre, across Tenth Street from Neighborhood Fellowship, was once the stage for in-person appearances by Bette Davis and Gloria Swanson. Built for glory in 1926, it was the first Universal Studios theater in Indiana.

3

The Neighborhood, Then and Now

Afternoon church services followed by free supper continued in the Strietelmeiers' living room for two years, and then the congregation moved to a storefront location for another two-and-a-half years. In 2000 Jim learned that the long-empty and nearly century-old First Reformed Church building, at 3102 E. Tenth Street, was for sale.

The First Reformed congregation originally called itself Hope Reformed Church before becoming Butler Memorial Church. In 1907 it moved to the Tenth Street location and changed names again to First Reformed Church. The Revival-style building with Arts and Crafts features was dedicated the following year, and an education wing was added in 1928.

In those turn-of-the-century days, the neighborhood was thriving with newcomers, many of them German immigrants with a penchant for culture and entertainment. The glitzy Spanish Mission-style Rivoli theater across the street from the Reformed Church opened in 1928 and could seat fifteen hundred people. It was the first Universal Studios theater built in Indiana, and its patrons reveled in such luxuries as ivory bathroom fixtures, leaded glass windows and copper lighting fixtures. A domed ceiling and two organ chambers made it the state's top-shelf home to theatrical performances and moving pictures. Stars such as Bette Davis and Gloria Swanson appeared there in person during Hollywood's golden age. In the Rivoli's waning years—the 1980s—rockers Bruce Springsteen and John Mellencamp gave live performances within those walls. Nowadays, the prostitutes and the destitute slouch against the Rivoli's boarded-up brick shell, which is all that remains of the splendor that used to be.

***

Woodruff Place, bordered by east Tenth and east Michigan Streets, was platted in 1872 by James O. Woodruff, who came to Indianapolis in 1869 to start the Indianapolis Water Company. Aside from the fact that the wealthy executive was looking for something to do with his money, he wanted to move his family outside the city. In those days, east Tenth filled the bill, so Woodruff platted his new neighborhood with sweeping, divided boulevards, sculptures and lush landscaping—thus, one of the first suburbs in the nation came to be.

The prominent residents who moved into Woodruff Place included author Booth Tarkington. Tarkington went on to write the Pulitzer Prize-winning *The Magnificent Ambersons*, and the Amberson Addition neighborhood described in the book is said to be based on Woodruff Place.

The neighborhood's population hit its high point in the 1950s and then began to decline, leaving the stately homes to be rented or divided into apartments. In fact, things got so low that in the mid-1970s, one once-noble house became the headquarters for the Outlaws motorcycle gang.

Salvation came later in the '70s when Woodruff Place

was named to the National Register of Historic Places. With many homes restored, it has regained part of its original splendor with new families moving in—including one family that moved there to volunteer at Neighborhood Fellowship. The irony of it all is that this original posh suburb went to rack and ruin, only to have suburbanites move back in, decades later, right next door to the poverty-stricken area of Tenth and Rural.

***

As the successful people moved out and the poor moved in during the 1960s and '70s, the Rivoli Theater deteriorated, finally closing in 1992. But rumor has it that renovations are on the horizon to restore the theater to its glory days. In 2004, the structure was designated an Indiana Historic Site, so the rumor may well be true. For now, the rusted marquee out front bears this message: "Support your local police."

The members of First Reformed Church worshipped across the street from the Rivoli until the 1970s when they merged with another church and left the building. It sat empty and deteriorating until Jim Strietelmeier found out about it. In fact, Jim collects churches, and later found the means to obtain another, which became Olive Branch Church in Broad Ripple. A congregation whose church closed in Kirklin, Indiana, donated the old building on the rural property to Neighborhood Fellowship.

The people of Zionsville Fellowship church put up the down payment for the First Reformed building, and by 2001, Neighborhood Fellowship had found a new home. Some who had committed to support Neighborhood Fellowship from the first days in the Strietelmeiers' living room continued coming to Sunday services in the century-old structure. They sang worship songs amid the cracking plaster and peeling paint. They stood, swaying and singing, on creaking wooden floors caked with a decade of grime. The ancient boiler groaned like a behemoth from the cavernous basement, but nobody seemed to care. They enjoyed their God-given gift, ignoring the enormity of making the rooms in the education wing useable. God would send help.

***

In the days to come, Neighborhood Fellowship faced a threatening trial in the form of eminent domain. In late 2002, the Indianapolis Public Schools District set its sights on the church property for a new elementary school. The district planned to demolish the 83-year-old IPS School No. 54, next door to Neighborhood Fellowship, and build an expanded elementary.

Barry Glaser went to a school board meeting and found plans for the new $13.2 million school. He asked about Neighborhood Fellowship, and was told school officials had talked to the "owners of the church" and that the building would be demolished by spring. Oh, really?

Barry called Jim.

That surprising bit of news, Jim said with a laugh, "disheartened us greatly."

The Strietelmeiers, Jacksons and Glasers had come too far to take this sitting down. They began praying. An attorney with a high-powered law firm who volunteered at the church, took the case for free. Others found out about their plight and got involved in saving the Neighborhood Fellowship ministry.

They relied on the Bible's ancient words for direction in this modern-day ordeal. "The book of Romans says, 'Bless those who curse you,'" Jim said, recalling that they were all but being cursed during that time of trials—literal trials in the courtroom.

School officials made noises about making an offer, but

none was ever made. The congregation would have said, "No thanks," anyhow. The *Indianapolis Star* followed the struggle, and one news story strangely warned that the case could go to court "if church members continue to reject IPS' offer." What offer?

"We were willing to move, if they could find another place for us," Jim said. "I explained that, because of our congregation and their needs, it would have to be within a mile of that building." People in the congregation don't have cars, he explained.

The IPS response: "That's not our problem."

Jim remembers the times he'd come out of a meeting and say to himself, "I've wrestled the bear."

Neighborhood Fellowship's plight went national. The conservative non-profit Alliance Defense Fund, based in Washington DC, said, "We are going to settle this in court, with a law that will affect 16 other states."

What? Change laws? Indiana Supreme Court? The ever-smiling Jim now was not happy. "It was all a distraction from what we were trying to do," he lamented.

The Historic Landmarks of Indiana and the Near-Eastside Community Organization got involved to save the old church building.

In the end, IPS backed off and built Brookside Elementary School No. 54 next door to the church building—in a school district whose students' average standardized test score in 2009 was in the failing 47.7 percentile range out of a possible 100, and a walloping 89 percent of students participate in the free lunch program. To get an idea of the dire need down at Tenth and Rural streets, compare those numbers to the Zionsville School Corporation's 2009 standardized test average of 90+ percentile and 3 percent of students participating in the free lunch program.

***

As it stands today, the Neighborhood Fellowship building's cracked walls have been repaired and painted, and new windows installed. A new projector hangs from the sanctuary ceiling to beam the words to worship songs onto a huge screen for all to see. New lighting floods the sanctuary. The floors are varnished and polished to a high shine. Still, this isn't "high church." A former horse trough still serves as a baptismal. But now it has a nice wood platform and surround made of materials pulled from the crawl space. Water for the trough comes through a garden hose attached directly to the water heater.

The academy has seen similar changes, with a library and second school room refurbished on the second floor. In 2008, classes were then moved to the top floor. The former academy classrooms now house, among other outreaches, a free clinic staffed by volunteers from the Indiana University Medical School.

***

Sources

http://www.broadripplehistory.com/ by Alan Haque
Lost Indianapolis by John P. McDonald
The Indianapolis Star
Indiana Department of Education

Former motorcycle gang enforcer Charles Riggle, known as "Sticks" until last year, serves up some mystery food in the cafeteria at Neighborhood Academy. He also answered to the name Lunch Lady, a moniker attached to him by the kids at the school.

4

Sticks

Jim greets me with one of those "Oh-well" smiles in the hallway at school. About a half-hour later, he tells me matter-of-factly that his cell phone and laptop were stolen that morning.

Jim isn't surprised anymore that thieves stop in regularly. They aren't all that picky, either, because they will take anything from bedding plants to musical instruments. One inventive type toted off a stained glass window in broad daylight while blending in with workmen installing new windows.

There's more to this than theft of belongings. Dealing with thievery steals Jim's time. But the worst theft, in both our opinions, is from children in poor neighborhoods who will inevitably have the irreplaceable gifts of innocence and security snatched from them. Creepy, degenerate people lurk all around these children. I remember the day Michelle, Abigail, Emily, John, Elizabeth, Will and the other kids were there when a prostitute brought her customer inside the church to do business in a closet. Neighborhood Academy students were robbed every time they watched from the windows as Jim dealt with junkies hawking drugs and sex from the church steps.

There was a time the church elders wanted to keep the building's doors open on weekdays, to help people such as these. How, they asked, can you minister through locked doors? They don't ask that anymore, mainly because there is no good answer. Yes, you can minister without musical instruments, stained glass windows, cell phones and laptops—all stolen through unlocked doors.

But no, you can't minister when you are a serial victim because of unlocked doors. Victimhood is seen as weakness in this neighborhood. No, you can't minister when your main job becomes policing a huge, ungainly building with plenty of hidden spaces that thieves, dopers and prostitutes think are their corporate headquarters. Not much time is left for ministry when your secondary job is filing police reports.

And so, the church doors were locked after that Thursday morning when the phone and laptop were stolen. For a while, on days I drove to the school, I would just pound on the door until someone came to open it. Soon, someone taped a sheet of paper to the window directing people to call a phone number so someone would come down and open the door. Now, they've gone high-tech. There's a doorbell.

Jim won't tell Charles Steven Riggle, better known as "Sticks," about the latest phone and laptop theft, because Sticks would likely break the person's neck if he ever found out who it was. I first met Sticks when I walked downstairs to the cafeteria one day to see if anyone needed help cleaning up after lunch. There, I saw a giant man sporting a bright red mohawk rhythmically shoving a wet mop over the concrete floor. Suddenly, the basement seemed ancient and menacing.

"Um, excuse me," I said, realizing too late that I was

vainly trying to sound brave—and for what? I'm just like the others who come down here and think that a basement and a man with a mop add up to a prickly state of affairs.

Slowly he turned, a looming, sinewy mass of tattoos and old clothes along with the problematic mohawk and teeth that probably hadn't seen a dentist's pick in a lifetime. He flashed a sympathetic street smile. By that I mean he was proud to be the source of my uneasiness. Superiority was his.

I tried to act nonchalant—you know, calm, cool, and collected. The man looked to be in his fifties, his face hardened and lined.

Jim rounded the corner just in time to make introductions. Sticks and I shook hands, eyeing each other with suspicion—except that Sticks was openly suspicious. I kept up the calm/cool act. It would be weeks before I trusted Sticks and longer before he trusted me. It was months before the two of us reached the cautious perimeter of friendship.

Sticks at that time worked at the church cleaning up, guarding the building at night and serving lunch to the kids. They called him the Lunch Lady. He had names for them, too, such as Fall-down Will. Name-calling meant they had bonded.

One day, long after I stopped being cool but long before he trusted me, Sticks and I were talking—or rather, he was putting up with my questions. I appreciated it. Jim was sitting there, too. Sticks said he tells the kids, "Instead of hitting someone, go hit a concrete wall. Bust up your own hand. It will later remind you that you were glad to smash yourself and not someone else's head."

"That advice doesn't work with these kids," Jim said, laughing.

I disagreed, thinking I should offer encouragement to

Sticks. Me, the writer, offering encouragement to Sticks the janitor. Like he really needed my help.

"No," I said, "Sticks's advice was good for the kids." My heart jumped when he wheeled and glared at me.

"I'll say this once," he said, pointing a finger in my face, which was by now beet red. "This is not advice. These kids go where they gotta go."

He had understood Jim's remark, and I had not. Jim was saying you can tell these kids a lot of things, but that doesn't mean they'll respect what you say, or that their circumstances can even allow them to do what you say. Sometimes, around here, you may have to hit a person, not a wall, to survive. As Sticks said, these kids "go where they gotta go."

Remembering that downtown rules are different from uptown rules, I didn't hang my head. I looked right back at Sticks, respecting his anger and taking the scolding as my due.

Suddenly, his anger gone as quickly as it had flared, Sticks declared, "You can give them love. That works. And give them food."

***

Life wasn't always like this for Sticks—guarding a church and joshing with kids.

He grew up on Indianapolis' south side. At age 14 he learned who his father was: "He was my mother's boyfriend."

He dropped out of Southport High School when he was 17 and joined the army during the Vietnam War. All he would say about that was, "At least now you know what you're suffering for, and it ain't so bad. It's your soul you should worry about."

For all of his scars, both inside and out, Sticks doesn't see that he's had a hard life.

He was once associated with Dick Leach, leader of the infamous Outlaws gang in Indianapolis. He worked as an enforcer, which means he enforced rules such as not stealing another gang member's motorcycle. He used the words bounty hunter and bouncer to describe his employment history.

"I stayed drunk for 12 years," said.

Once, Sticks passed out drunk while on watch detail outside a bar, and someone stole a gang member's motorcycle. He had broken the rule of enforcing the rules, and the Outlaws told him he had two options: get out of town or go to the basement and take his punishment.

"I was the one who fell asleep. It was my fault. I respected that," Sticks said. "Being a soldier of that world, I went down to the basement with those guys to take what was coming to me. They tied me up with my feet and hands behind a chair and beat me with a phone book."

Three guys whaled at him with that phone book for a good fifteen minutes, breaking his nose. Blood spurted from his eyes, ears, and mouth. Then, they loaded him into a van and took him to someone's apartment, where a lady nursed him back to health.

"After that, they had respect for me, because I took my dues," he said. In his world, this was not violence but an educating moment. He continued working security for gangs, night clubs, and strip joints, but he never again passed out on the job.

***

Back to the day of the laptop/cell phone theft. If Sticks ever found the thieves, he'd threaten to tear their heads off or at least beat them with a phone book. Jim says that knowing about the robbery would rob Sticks of his joy.

Despite Jim's earnest intentions, word gets to Sticks about the robbery. Though he has sworn off his old life and has become a follower of Jesus Christ, the old cultural thought patterns persist.

He is mopping the basement floor at the church when he tells me he knows.

"So," I ask, "What do you think? Jim says knowing about this would rob you of your joy."

"I'd have joy putting my hands around that person's neck. I can't help who I am."

He silently, furiously mops on. I back off.

Crime is always a joy robber. It's the same for people in the suburbs, only, I suppose, on a different level, since everyone has insurance. But the fact is, no one is immune. You can't be good enough or faithful enough to escape thieves. Nobody deserves them, and everybody's vulnerable.

A thief at my parents' house bagged my mother's wedding rings. We were robbed of $30 at our own garage sale by a man in a yellow Cadillac. A man once kicked in the door to my office at the shopping center in the middle of the night and made off with lots of stuff. Thieves once took the air conditioning equipment from the top of my brother-in-law's art supply store. My cousin who is legally blind was brutally assaulted and robbed at a bus stop. If all of this is just in my one little life, imagine the millions of others who suffer at the hands of those who rob them of their possessions, their security, and their innocence.

Still, the hope is that guilt will find those who steal. We hope for repentance and restitution. It seems a forlorn hope. Four years have passed since that exchange with Sticks in the church basement, and the computer and phone are still gone, as are the musical instruments, the stained glass window, the lawn mowers, and myriad other things stolen—most comically a couple of roosters from Jim's backyard.

As Jim says, "If we don't laugh, we'll cry." The roosters were last seen in the spring of 2008 by a neighbor who reported a person in a big hat making off down the alley "with a large, flapping plastic bag." Jim did manage to track down and retrieve his stolen van, though. There was no guilty conscience on the part of the thief.

***

Sticks calls his tattoos memorial body art. They belie his assertion that his life has not been hard. Sticks being Sticks, he decides shock me, so he rolls down his lower lip to reveal a tattooed slogan: Eat me. He proudly states that he wouldn't show me what was under his top lip.

"Good choice," I say.

I don't want to hurt Sticks's feelings, so I don't let on at first that I've seen worse, back in the 1980s when I covered cops and courts for the *The Lebanon Reporter* up in Boone County. Lebanon is the county seat, where the major crimes were bar fights and drunken brawls involving perpetually downcast couples who were sick of each other. But talking to Sticks prompted memories of a gang member who came too far north from Indianapolis to cover up his crime and ended up in the Boone County Jail. I was assigned to the story. There had been a killing in Indianapolis, and the body of Outlaws motorcycle gang member David "Pigpen" Lakes wound up dumped in Boone County ditch between Lebanon and Zionsville. The body was hauled off to the coroner's office for an autopsy.

The cops back then were forever telling me sordid details of local crime scenes, gleeful when I was shocked and horrified. I learned quickly to register mild dismay. But mild dismay was impossible the day they rolled out

Pigpen Lakes's autopsy photos when I showed up on my daily newsgathering rounds.

My mind returns to the present, and Sticks is asking me about the worst crime I covered in my newspaper days. And so I tell him about murder and mayhem involving gang members David "Pigpen" Lakes and Steven "The Weed" Weaver.

After police arrested Steven "The Weed" and his wife for Lakes's murder, the Weed was so ruthless that he shot his wife to keep her from talking. She still talked—from a wheelchair because the bullet had forever damaged her spinal cord. I had to cover that trial, and I hated doing it because of the sheer evilness of the crime. Christians don't belong around such evil, I thought.

Sticks, it turns out, knew both the victim and the killer from his former gang days. "David was a pretty good guy," he says of Pigpen. "He watched out for children and respected old people." Sticks doesn't have much to say about Weed Weaver.

He is impressed that I had covered the murder trial. Hence, I bask in newfound respect. It strikes me that we can be connected to people we hardly know by the thinnest of filaments, some so fine and fragile they get buried on the backside of the complicated tapestry of life—to paraphrase author Edith Schaffer. But God knows the thread is there, for He has woven it into time and space, to be revealed at just this moment. This is the start of my friendship with Sticks.

We Christians shouldn't tell ourselves that we don't belong around such evil, for this is often where God does His mightiest of works.

***

Sticks's body art memorials include a jailhouse tattoo on his neck: R.I.P. Mom. The words "Dad the best" and "Hell" are written on his hands, along with the crudely-etched number 4427. That's the address of a pal from the Outlaws gang. The long, involved explanation for that one boils down to the fact that Sticks was going to take a driving test for the man, which means he had to memorize his friend's address. So he tattooed the address on his hand.

Sticks wants to make it clear that he was never a bona-fide Outlaws member, but was a freelance enforcer: "I just worked for them. There was one guy we caught in the parking lot and put him in the (car) trunk and took him to the railroad tracks. A train was coming. He was crying and wet his pants. We pulled him off at the last minute and then we told him, 'If we see you here again, we'll kill you.'"

"I chose that life," he said. "My daddy didn't raise me to do that."

Philosophical to the bone, Sticks declares that the railroad track incident had been an educating moment for the young man: "That kid left the gang life and went back to school."

Sticks's left arm bears images of ships, his right an eagle. Blue tears are crudely etched on his cheek, beneath his right eye. A jailhouse tattoo is written above the third tear. It says T-2.

"Those are tears for the dead, one that I killed," he says. He won't tell me any more, and Jim later says not to bother asking again. I didn't, until about a year later, when Sticks brought up the tears. I find him working around the cafeteria, unwilling to sit down. He just keeps working and talking. Talking and putting the potato chips away. Talking and wiping tables. He wants to tell me about the tears. The first tear, he says, cries for his mother. She had Alzheimer's. Number two is for his father, "For all he went through, taking care of my mother." Number three is in memory of T-2, his dog.

I am quietly glad Sticks tells me about the tears, and about T-2, the one he said he killed because T-2 "was suffering," and Sticks had to put him down. Jim says not to believe all of Stick's explanations, but one thing is a fact: Jim did T-2's funeral in the middle of the night. He found himself and some other gang types drinking a toast to the dog—straight from T-2's water dish. When it's the middle of the night in a strange house with strange people, you just do what they say, Jim said.

For now, Sticks says, he's glad he's in the neighborhood, because "This is my war zone. The kids feel safe here at school. I've always had a purpose, it's just that my tour of duty has changed. This is my last tour. I do it for the Lord, and it counts."

I saw Sticks recently in the basement at lunchtime when a little boy named Craig was acting up. Sticks ordered Craig to his side and the kid stalwartly saluted while Sticks gave him a stern lecture on behavior. "Got that?" he barked, drill-sergeant style. "Yes *sir,*" Craig barked back before snapping the salute and running back to play and behave himself.

***

In 2006, Sticks started coughing up blood. On April 27 of that year a biopsy of a spot on his lung showed cancer. The people of Neighborhood Fellowship rallied, taking him to and from his doctor appointments. That's when he moved into the building to live—for a while.

The trouble unleashed by cancer seemed to be more than he could bear. He went back to drinking and, as others have done, he disappeared from the church rather than face the hard call of obedience to Jesus Christ. Sometimes, the kids still see him across the street outside the Laundromat.

And so, my pages of notes on Sticks abruptly end. What remains in my notebook are three things he said that I call Sticks-isms. Here are my two favorites:

Here's a three-step rule from my bar-bouncing days, when people just kept doing what they were doing and I had to throw them out: 1. They may not have heard you. 2. They may not have understood you. 3. They're saying (expletive deleted). It's the same way in life.

The cousin to vulgarity is violence. If you hear a bunch of vulgarity, violence is hovering around.

***

I only wish Sticks knew how smart he is, and that God is using him on these pages to stir someone to hope and to repentance. That same year, we all prayed for his return, with confidence he would come back, for the Lord's good work was just begun in him.

Beth Alsmeyer reads on the library couch with Stefon and Craig in 2009. Beth and her husband, Aaron, oversee Neighborhood Academy, along with Jesse Glaser.

5

The Others

Dozens of people teach, tutor and intern at Neighborhood Fellowship for no pay. Volunteers also come here to serve food on Sundays, help with cleanup, do construction and just lend moral support. Others deliver furniture, food and clothing. Medical students provide free care at Saturday clinics. People who know their way around a ledger come to do the accounting and book work. Some have moved downtown, and some drive down on a daily or weekly basis. One retired music teacher spent several years teaching music to the youngsters and encouraging Jim and Debbie.

People who aren't "regulars" at the school have formed bonds with the kids, acting as prayer partners over the school year. They bring and send little gifts, but their greatest offering is the prayer and the encouragement that someone cares.

In the early days, a group of men who call themselves Friends of the 'Hood tore out walls, put in walls, hammered, painted, and sweated to get the Strietelmeirs' house on North Beville in shape. Later, they similarly labored at the church building. They help with administrative matters. Different people come every Sunday to serve the free meal offered after services, and to help clean up. Some have said the people getting the free meals should clean up. But getting people downtown to partner with the ministry and become familiar with it has its own value.

On any given day I'm there, I see someone from Zionsville Fellowship. I learn that someone helped with a play, or someone is signing up volunteers to teach Vacation Bible School, or someone with a truck will haul your used furniture to the church. I had a couch to give away, and Jim told me to just have Roger Graham deliver it to the church. He predicted someone would take it home the very day it arrived. He was right, of course.

It is utterly amazing to see the number of people involved in Neighborhood Academy. Jim doesn't count heads, so I started a list. The list just kept growing and, as time went on, I knew there would be others beyond others. For all the people who have abandoned these kids, there are many others who are faithful. I'll mention the career volunteers here, with apology to those others whose names aren't listed, knowing that God sees their labors.

Mike and Cindi Hale were the first Neighborhood Fellowship family to adopt children they were foster parenting. Others have followed suit, obtaining foster-care licenses to rescue children from the brokenness in which they live. The Hales started fostering in 2003 when sisters Christina, three, and Kimberly, two, came to live with them, followed in 2005 by their other siblings Jessica and Isaiah, who were babies. The adoption was final in October 2008, and four children make for lots of commotion in the Hale home on Tecumseh Street—about three blocks from the Strietlemeiers'. A "masseuse" lives across the street. There are always really nice cars in that driveway. Another neighbor howls at the moon, sometimes. The Hales love their neighbors and interact with them in helpful ways.

"We feel that missionaries are to go in and grow with the culture," Cindi said. "We have more experience than if we had just come in to 'fix the people.' We are intentional about relationships."

They'd like to adopt more kids, but Cindi says, "We need to get things in order here, first." They're working hard with Christina, who Cindy says is diagnosed with obsessive compulsive disorder.

Christina is now eight. She comes onto the porch wearing a helmet and saying she wants to ride her bike. Mike puts an arm around her and says, "In a little while, okay?"

We talk at length about the days Mike and Cindi met at Trinity College in Chicago and later were in the same small group from Eagle Creek Fellowship, which would become the core congregation for Neighborhood Fellowship. Mike is an elder at Neighborhood and works with the youth. The Hales say they used to pick up kids from Cindi's club at Wheeler and bring them to Neighborhood Fellowship.

Christina still wants to ride her bike. Mike tells about the time he and the kids were at a local drive-through and noticed a holdup going on inside. He called 911 and was put on hold, complete with Muzak. As he waited on hold, the gunmen emerged with their booty and saw Mike, through the windshield, on the cell phone. He put the car in reverse and hit the gas.

Christina now has her bike helmet on. We finish our conversation, and she skips off toward her bicycle, holding tight to Mike's hand, the other holding tight to that helmet.

***

Barry and Jessie Glaser are foster parents who also take care of other people's foster children. Then, they go on to adopt more kids. When their niece, Crystal, had troubles at home and at Broad Ripple High School, they brought her to Neighborhood Academy.

Jessie is up at 5:00 AM for some alone time before she gets her foster daughter up at 6:00. Then, she awakens her own five in time to get to school. Three neighbor kids come over before school to wait for a ride. Those three are in foster care because their parents are in jail.

"I offered our home for the three kids so their foster parents could go to work and they wouldn't have to worry," Jessie says, matter-of-factly.

She and Barry are tortured by the knowledge that there are two ways things can go for these little ones: either they can be adopted or be pulled away from their foster family and sent back into the system at the state's whim. Adoption means the birth parents must relinquish all parental rights. Being put back into the system means the child will disappear from the Glasers' lives and from Neighborhood Fellowship.

"Many's the time we've asked God, 'What do you want us to do?'" Jessie tells me, her face pained, but then brightening. "Then we remember that God adopts all those who come to Him."

The Glasers live out the command to care for widows and orphans. They may want to keep all of their foster children, but they know the limitations. Still, two more foster children—Craig and Timmy—would be placed with the Glasers in 2007, their mother pregnant with a third child.

"We are adopting these two and, oh, I hope we get the baby, too," Jessie says during a party held later in 2008 to celebrate the Strietelmeiers' adoption of Michelle and Jacob.

She and Barry still say to themselves, "Just one more. We can help one more."

***

Robin McEwan was a CPA before she started coming to the Academy to help out in the classroom in January of 2005. When kids needed help, she was there. If Jessie needed help, she was there.

Like the rest of us who bring our cultures to foreign places, Robin assumed the kids would treat her with respect because she was an adult. They didn't overtly disrespect her; they just accepted her presence with sidelong glances and sluggish indifference. These kids aren't impressed just because you show up in their class one day and smile at them. They aren't impressed if you go back for several months. Don't even imagine that they will think you are cool because you know some kid lingo. What they are, because so many people have come and gone in their lives, is suspicious. To them, Robin was just another looming person, another kindly face from the other side of town. Here today, gone tomorrow.

But Robin stayed. The more she was around Kim, Rachel, Will, John and the others, she found she couldn't stay away. Looking back, she sees that her task would have been impossible if she saw it as a "duty to the poor."

"You have to be down here because you have a heart for these people," she told me one day after class. "You have to be called. I definitely feel called to be down here. What else could I do? I wasn't going to go out and play tennis."

She started tutoring Michelle and Beth in English and took over the younger class in 2006 after the class was divided. She and her husband, Ken, had just finished remodeling their suburban home when they decided to move downtown to Woodruff Place so she could be closer to work. In 2009, she's going for a degree in elementary education.

"She's no longer with us," Jim says. "But we are thankful she came through here."

***

Kate and Eric Scott and their two young children live in the parsonage next door to the church. A family from Zionsville Fellowship wrangled the purchase of the house, a neglected mess of dank smells, rotting wood and grime. Gary Henry, a Friend of the 'Hood, got construction materials, and Vince and Kara Ranieri gave cabinets from their kitchen to fix up the place for the Scotts. Eric started as a two-year intern for Neighborhood Fellowship while working at a coffee shop. Kate does babysitting.

***

Doug and Joy Elliott were there from the start and, Jim says, "were always the tail wagging the dog." One day as she loaded things into her car, Joy Elliott said to Jim, "We should start a school."

Jim replied, "Are you out of your mind?"

From that insanity sprang the first roots of Neighborhood Academy. It's operated under the Accelerated Christian Education curriculum, under which the students work independently, with the teacher checking their work at intervals during the day.

They continue their work today with school, foster care, and myriad other aspects of Neighborhood Fellowship.

***

Then, there's the Alsmeyer family. I couldn't go downtown the winters of 2006–09 without seeing Judy Alsmeyer sitting on a chair in the middle of the classroom, as Robin McEwan had done, watching and waiting to help a student. Sometimes Phil Jackson occupied that chair, but it was mostly Judy. It was the go-to chair. Someone need a paper checked? Go to The Chair. Someone doesn't get a story problem? Go to The Chair. Sometimes, the kids raise a flag to indicate they need help, and Judy goes to their desks.

A few times when there was an English question, such as, "is this a definite article, and should it be used in an imperative sentence with an implied subject?" Judy would say, "Leslie's here. She'll probably know the answer to that." Not likely. On the whole, English majors who aren't teachers have long forgotten the glossary of terms for sentence structure. Still, by the end of the year, these kids knew their modal auxiliaries from their prepositions.

I met Judy's son, Aaron, when he was rehearsing *The King and I* with the kids. He was a Butler University senior at the time and had brought a group of homeschoolers to Neighborhood Academy to be in the cast, the idea being to bring the two groups of students together. It was a great idea, but I saw that outside of the actual rehearsing, Academy kids huddled with Academy kids and homeschoolers huddled with homeschoolers, sort of like the boy-girl segregations at junior high school dances—except when they all played basketball in the gym after practice.

The Neighborhood Academy kids were proud of their roles. Crystal was involved behind the scenes. John was playing the ship captain. James had a speaking part. Rachel, of course, had the happy role of singing and dancing in the chorus, as did Michelle and Elizabeth.

Singing and laughter blend with strains of "happy talk" as I approach the rehearsal room. A month into practice, lines have been memorized and yards of material donated for costumes. I ask how things were going.

"We aren't doing the play," Crystal says.

It all began to crumble when the kids learned that one of the scenes called for them to bow down to Buddha.

They couldn't bring themselves, as committed Christians, to do that, even if it was play-acting. On their behalf, Aaron wrote to the Rodgers and Hammerstein organization to see whether they could delete that scene. The answer was no. Aaron let the cast decide, and the kids voted to scrap the whole thing.

But Aaron and his girlfriend, Beth Walsman, didn't scrap the idea of a production. They wrote a musical, *Esther*, which played in May 2008 at the University of Indianapolis, casted with homeschoolers and Neighborhood Academy and accompanied by a nine-piece orchestra. John, James, Rachel, Abigail, Elizabeth, and Michelle were onstage and other kids acted as stagehands. Judy Alsmeyer made a good number of the costumes. It was a packed house the night I went. What I saw more than matched anything I had seen in my years working in amateur theater or in any high school production. I was amazed at the writers' detail and talent, not to mention the actors' professionalism and dedication. After the two-and-a-half-hour production was over and everyone was mixing it up in the lobby, I told James, "I fully expect to see you on Broadway."

Judy Alsmeyer's first year at Neighborhood Academy was 2003. Her introduction to the school came through an effort to guide her daughter, Kristy. Kristy Alsmeyer had told her mother she was thinking about volunteering at a women's shelter.

Dismayed, Judy found herself thinking, *Kristy doesn't know a thing about ministering to battered women.*

She suggested that Kristy take her missionary calling to Neighborhood Fellowship. Kristy went to check it out, and Judy went along. "I decided, on the spot, to stay," Judy would later tell me.

It was a harder decision for Kristy. At age 18, she had envisioned overseas missionary work and didn't particularly want to work at the school. But as God would have it, she did begin working there and a year later moved in with Jim and Debbie.

"I had to do what God was calling me to do," she says. "To be the salt and light of the Earth."

Kristy recalls that her decision brought on attacks spiritual warfare. Health problems and the loss of comforts bothered her. She soldiered on, and God honored her faithfulness.

She is now married to playwright Beth Walsman's brother, Joel. Joel is an electrician, and Kristy is expecting her second baby. They live eight doors down from the Strietelmeiers on Beville Avenue and devote hours to Neighborhood Academy.

As for Judy, the school may have been a love at first sight, but the kids—Holly, Kim, Hope, Jacob, and the others—took a while to warm up to her. A breakthrough came the day she saw Holly working on a scrapbook.

"Oh, you like to scrapbook?"

Holly, sarcastically, said, "Yeah."

Judy replied, "Kristy likes to scrapbook too. Can I show you some of her pictures?"

Holly was willing, and Judy brought in some scrapbooks. The two had found common ground in a simple task.

Like many of the others, Judy went to work here thinking about how to fix the problems in the children's lives. Like the rest of us, she learned the truth, that there's a bottomless pit of need in the lives of the poor; that fixing the problems isn't always possible, and it's definitely not always the answer.

She concentrated on helping nurture spiritual freedom through Christianity. At least the children would have that. In fact, spiritual healing doesn't necessarily mean solved problems or a change of location.

But with spiritual healing comes the ability to stop

damaging themselves, to cope with what is, and to learn to be overcomers to the extent their talents, backgrounds, and personalities will allow. The hope lies in letting them find joy and the love of Christ in the midst of their sorrows and leaving the rest to Him. Sometimes, just having someone like Judy there eases their pain or gives them a bit of security before they go back home. And that's the fixing they are going to have.

"It's way too big for any of us," Judy says. "But you can reach them, one kid at a time."

Moses Strietelmeier gets some help from Aaron Alsmeyer.

6

Visits to the School

The year is 2005. Trudging up the time-worn steps to the Neighborhood Academy classroom, you look forward to getting there because suddenly, you'll be in a brighter place where walls are painted a warm, creamy yellow, old light fixtures have been replaced by ceiling fans, and there's new, wall-to-wall school-grade carpeting on the floor.

The classroom has an excited buzz today, what with the new windows and clear view. A reading area sports a bright rug, a couple of sofas, and shelves of donated books—old standards, from Nancy Drew mysteries and Pipi Longstocking tales to *Anne of Green Gables* and Sinclair Lewis's *Main Street.*

"We prefer the classics," Jim says, also pointing to C.S. Lewis's *The Chronicles of Narnia* and Victor Hugo's *The Hunchback of Notre Dame.* There's a series of books full of Bible stories, next to a row of Bibles and books by theologians Oswald Chambers, Francis Shaffer, and G. K. Chesterton. To the right are ten volumes of *Discover Science.*

Simple cubicles lining the walls carve out each child's

own corner of the education world and provide little plywood shelters from their hard lives outside this building.

Johnny, ten, is small for his age. He limps along on palsied legs, holding up his pants in the back with his good hand. He came here after having been "mainstreamed" into elementary-age classes in Indianapolis Public Schools. He didn't know his alphabet his first day at Neighborhood Academy in 2004. A year later, he's reading at first-grade level.

When it's time to tackle the flight of stairs on the way to lunch or to the playground, Johnny hops matter-of-factly onto one of the older boys' backs. On the playground, his sisters, Hope and Kelly, lift him into a tire swing hung from a tree. It's just what they do. No heaving, no comment, just a routine lifting, shifting his legs so he's comfortable, giving the tire a spinning push, and then turning back to what they were doing before.

There, Johnny swings and spins in gleeful freedom, a respite in the sunshine from his moment-by-moment drudgery of movement that will never go away. The tire slows, and no one spins it again. He waits for someone to notice him in the curve of the tire and lift him out. They do, and he emerges smiling and smelling rubbery.

"They're a package deal," explains Jim of the three siblings.

John is a quiet worker, big for his fifteen years, and often the object of jokes by the others. But the jokes are gentle, and John laughs along. He's seemingly undaunted by just one more tragedy of life: it's just been a year since his father died. All anyone knows is that it was a lung condition.

John's mother and Jessie grew up together, so here he is at Neighborhood Academy. "Caring for him," Jim says, "is one way we care for orphans and widows."

Kim stands, as usual, at the workbook counter,

thumbing to today's lesson and seriously tackling the work. You remember Kim—the girl with the story problem on the first page of this book. She is philosophical about maybe not graduating this year, and the teachers wonder if it's a comfort-zone thing. They tell her what she must do to move on, but she's sluggish about it. She's like the mother figure here, after all.

Kim's countenance shows worry, like that of a mother whose children's lives are a quagmire of endless troubles. She watches, corrects, and hopes. She also seethes. The younger ones look up to her, so she acts like she knows what she's doing; like she has answers for them. And sometimes, she does.

Then, there's 16-year-old Justin, Kim's best friend in the class. The kids call him Jofus, which is how his speech impediment allowed him to say Joseph as he studied the Bible account of the seriously maligned hero. Were it not for Neighborhood Academy, Justin would attend nearby Tech High School, where half the students drop out early in their high school years. If he graduates from Neighborhood Academy, he'll be the first in the family with a high school diploma. He's usually Johnny's ride down the stairs.

The smartest kid in the class could well be Jacob, a frisky ten-year-old who gets away with murder because he finishes his lessons early—when he agrees to do them. He can whip through six pages of math problems in the time it takes the others to do one. He doesn't make mistakes. In any other school, Jacob's social disability, Reactive Attachment Disorder, would be his front-and-center label. Here, he is nurtured as one of a little band of struggling people.

Jacob and his older sister, Michelle, are the only ones in a household of six children and several adults who are not mentally handicapped. Among the jumble of people they go home to each day, some are related, others are not.

In the near future, Child Protective Services will take Michelle and Jacob from their mother and put them in the county children's home. Like Kim, they are bound for suffering. It seems their little backs might collapse under the burdens no child should have to carry. But today they are happy at school, Michelle always smiling and willing for a hug, and Jacob always willing with a wisecrack.

Another vying for smartest-kid status is Gabby Glaser, Barry and Jessie's daughter. At fifteen, she has a servant's heart, Jessie says. "She puts others before herself, no matter what."

Gabby, her brother, Will, and sisters Rachel, Bethany, and Miriam come to school each day. The three foster children from across the street whose birth parents are in jail come over to wait at Neighborhood Fellowship for their public school to start nearby.

"Some of the ones we bring here are kids in trouble and some are our own," explains Jessie. She and Barry just keep bringing them home. They can't resist caring. Next year, Kourtney will come to them. By 2008, there will be up to four foster kids at a time in the Glaser home, and they will adopt most of them.

Rachel, 13, is the ringleader-artist of the group in 2005. She rallies the girls during recess to practice dance routines she has choreographed for a show at year's end. She makes promotional posters for the dance show and gets everyone to pitch in. Rachel is allowed to be herself, except for going barefoot. That's not allowed, Jessie tells her. After a good sulk, she puts on her shoes.

Bethany is 15 that same year and loves social studies. She could have gone to a charter school in Indianapolis, where children labeled at-risk are sent. "I like this better," she says, sitting at her cubicle, chewing on a worn-down nub of pencil. "You're more on your own, and you can get done with your work. You're also not sitting at a computer all day."

Fourteen-year-old Abigail Strietelmeier is serious. She likes to wear a headscarf, tied underneath her hair at the back of the neck. She is a Barnabas-type, bringing up the rear in dutiful solitude. She gets the food at lunchtime and helps clean up. On guitar lesson days, she stands patiently in the gray light at the front door of the church, peering through the dusty window, waiting for her ride.

Her sister, Elizabeth, at 12, is one of Rachel's dancers, eager to be in on things, wanting to please. Though dancing isn't her forte, she gives it her all. She has a better gift, though. It's called compassion. She sticks up for John when the others tease him at lunch.

Little Joseph Strietelmeier does his best to keep up with the pack as they race around the lunchroom and on the playground, but spends most afternoons asleep in a Pack & Play crib set up in the classroom. Debbie Strietelmeier is often multi-tasking in the classroom as mother of the preschooler and teacher to the older ones. Moses, their third-born, attends public school near home. Next year he will come to Neighborhood Fellowship.

After teaching a history class Jim runs off to tend to an emergency. Debbie goes over to Joseph in the Pack & Play because he needs help with his pants. Jessie looks up and sees on the monitor that there are some people downstairs who need food.

***

It may seem like people are aimlessly milling around the classroom this one spring day, but they know what they are doing. Gabby leafs through a shelf of workbook keys to check her own work. John sits, bending over his math problems, clumsily holding a pencil, his mouth in tight concentration.

Johnny is in the reading area, looking through a book about a monster. Michelle and Rachel lean around the ends of their cubicles for a gab and a giggle between long workbook stints. Jacob throws a paper wad at Will.

"Get to work, Jacob," says Jessie, not looking up from helping Justin at the teacher's table. She's one of those people who sees things without looking up. Moms like her used to say, "I have eyes in the back of my head." Jacob picks up his pencil, the snicker wiped from his face.

A young man who says his name is Vee walks in to ask when the GED classes are starting. "Thursday, Friday, and Saturday," says Jessie. He sniffs and asks for a Kleenex. I open my purse to get the tissue, and Jim moves in closer. Vee takes the tissue, eyeing Jim, and leaves. "It's never a good idea to open a purse too near a stranger around here," Jim says. Vee never did come back for the classes.

Now, it's time for a five-minute break. Kids play computer games, talk among themselves, and move around the room. Jacob gets to horse around, and Johnny capers over to join in the fun. The teenage girls gossip in a sunny corner by a window. John stays at his desk, still hunched over the math problems.

Fifteen minutes later, Jessie rings an old-fashioned school handbell. "Okay, everyone, back to your desks."

***

The kids have customized their plywood cubicles. Bethany's has a doll, a pencil basket and a cut-out picture of a Volkswagen Beetle. Across the top of Johnny's cubicle hangs a sling of paper squares and triangles from a past school project. Will's desk is a mess of stuff with no particular theme. Pencils, worksheets and random scraps of paper have stuck where they landed.

Kelly is all neatness and order, her cubicle walls festooned with a paper piano keyboard and a pink Bible sitting on a ledge. The pencils are in order, and a carefully crafted paper name card stakes her claim.

Jim helps Elizabeth with a math problem. "How many decimal points do we have to move?" He tries again: "How many dots over on this one?"

Then, it's on to Michelle: "Sixteen minus two is what?"

"Fifteen? ... um, no, fourteen."

Justin-Jofus stands waiting. He needs help working on fractions.

Gabby walks over to get one of the 1995 *World Book Encyclopedias* from the library shelf. Watching her pull a volume from the shelf calls up memories of yesterday's door-to-door salesmen whose Comptons, Americanas, and Brittanicas—complete with racks—were proudly set up in living rooms across America. A set of encyclopedias was just part of the furniture.

Fast-forward through computer CD encyclopedias to Wikipedia, if you're lucky. More often, students across America swear by online blathering as encyclopedic gospel. Term papers, any more, are mere regurgitations of online message board opinions and blog misquotes. But not at Neighborhood Academy. Here, they go to the encyclopedias of old and flip through the pages. The 1967 set is upstairs, Jim says.

Gabby takes the volume over to one of the six new donated classroom computers. Computers and old encyclopedias. A contrast, visible and disturbing, of need in the midst of plenty. High-tech hardware is perched on old wooden office desks hauled from some far-flung room in the big, old building. The desks, of course, are too high for the youngsters, forcing shoulders to hitch up and wrists to work above the prescribed elbow-level. Kids get cranky after being in such an uncomfortable position for any length of time. But no one has come in to point out that they really do need ergonomically correct computer stations, so the kids don't know why they're cranky.

***

Time for lunch, and everyone gets in a circle for prayer, led by Barry. It's chicken and noodles today, set out by Abigail and her mother. Johnny hops on Jofus's back, and Will gives someone a shove on the way down the two flights of stairs to the mess hall/gym/auditorium. Kim tells them to knock it off. Rachel flies happily down the stairs in her cool miniskirt and tights, oblivious to the raucous clamoring of the boys. It's time to hit the stage in the gym for dance practice after lunch.

A wild game of dodgeball takes over half the huge room before anyone actually sits down to eat chicken and noodles. John, Rachel, and Jofus are the champs as the younger ones squeal and dodge. College-age Beth Walsman and Kristy Alsmeyer have come in to help and play with the kids. Over at a table, someone helps Johnny with his spoon, which he grabs back so he can feed himself.

And there sits Kim, quietly, at another table, once again talking about maybe not graduating this year. She puts her head down on the table. Her concerns would prove true. The following September she will be back at Neighborhood Academy. Jim, sensing that she won't graduate this time, has an opinion: "When you're about to graduate and you've never had anyone tell you how to live, it's hard. We are trudging. We are committed, even if it kills her. She will graduate, in time."

Lunch is over, and Sticks is in the kitchen getting out the mop and bucket. That's a signal it's time to go upstairs. As I watch the unspoken command, I think of a waiter asking if he can bring the check because he knows it's time to turn the table.

Today, everyone gathers post-lunch in the old sanctuary to see the new audio-visual equipment for Sunday services. The arrival of the new projector—a gift from suburban churches—is cause for celebration. Videos and words to worship songs can now be projected onto a screen that descends by remote control from the ceiling. It beats the old overhead projector flashing words on worn-out transparencies onto the wall.

Reaching to the high, gothic ceiling, is a scaffold the workmen are using to affix the projector. Far below, Will is capering about, yanking on a rope attached to the scaffolding. Uh-oh. Other kids are playing "keep away" with John's baseball cap. A bar of the metal scaffolding falls, bonking Will on the head. He starts bawling. Nobody is noticing the new AV equipment.

Now it's off to the restroom before class restarts. The girls' room has a new, pink floor and new drywall on three walls, leaving the fourth peeling with plaster as though someone had a spurt of energy to make it nice, and then either left or gave up.

But oh, the new windows. You want to throw them open, just because you can, and because it's springtime. Never mind that on the day they were put in, thieves posing as installers walked out with a cherished ancient stained-glass window. There's plywood over the missing window, now. The following Sunday, someone will make off with the light fixtures on either side of the entrance.

***

In the suburbs, most classrooms have a TV monitor on the wall for the latest in visual learning. What the kids at Neighborhood Academy learn on their small, old tabletop classroom monitor is who is coming in or going out the side door. It's the door used by the thieves and prostitutes. But who wants to lock the doors against the very poor, destitute, desperate people the church was established to welcome?

Jessie monitors the monitor as she tutors the kids. She thinks about tomorrow and getting up for quiet time before the neighbor kids roll in to be taken to school. She gets up from her seat at the desk and takes up the old school bell. At its welcome ring, workbooks are dutifully put back on the shelves, cubicle chairs scooted in, and bread—donated each week by a fancy bread shop up north—grabbed to take home.

Outside, the kids pile into the donated Neighborhood Academy bus, and Jim drives everyone home.

***

In fall 2007, Crystal, James and Kourtney are no longer the newcomers they were the previous year. Gabby will graduate with honors in the spring and go on to Moody Bible Institute in Chicago. Jofus has dropped out, a casualty to wandering away from God and school. He's also a product of the neighborhood, where there were two murders in May. People on Tenth Street are afraid for their lives.

Jim and Phil asked Jofus for a specific apology for disrespect, and he complied but has not come back to school. They're giving him time to get right with God.

Crystal's father tried to kill her mother and went to prison. Later, after his release, he would come to church with the Strietelmeiers. But this is 2007, and Crystal can't live with her mother. She is living with a Neighborhood Fellowship family. I'm frantically tutoring her so that she can graduate this year. As we pore over Samuel Johnson and Alexander Pope's "Essay on Man," Crystal hums, taps her feet. and changes the subject to teenager things, like clothes.

I pull her back to the lesson. Sometimes, over the weeks of tutoring, she has to correct me! When this happens, I say, "That was a test." We laugh. In the end she learns, passes the exams, and graduates with hopes of going on a summer mission trip, attending classes at Crossroads Bible College, and eventually teaching.

"I have trouble with temptation," she tells me one day as we go over Oliver Goldsmith's pastoral poem, "The Deserted Village." She is talking about the temptation to be cool, and all of the debauchery it takes to earn the title. "It's better for me to be here."

At Broad Ripple High, where she attended before moving downtown, there were fashion wars, cliques, girl fights, and boys wanting sex. Here, everyone gets along, she says. These days, when she gets dressed in the morning, she bends forward in front of the mirror to check out the view. "If I see anything I would not want my grandfather to see, I change clothes."

She works on her graduation speech. I listen and she reads the speech while fidgeting at a music-stand podium. I tell her about eye contact and voice inflection. The next time she reads, there's no eye contact and no inflection. After two weeks of no eye contact and no inflection, Crystal can look up from her notes when she talks. She looks right at me. It's a week before graduation, and she doesn't like any of this speech stuff. But she does it anyway. The best line in her speech is, "For the first time in my life, I'm being Crystal."

***

Kourtney, who is living with the Glasers, ran away from her last foster home. She has to be told she cannot listen to a crude local radio show on the computer. "That kind of stuff is banned from our homes, our cars, our lives," Jessie tells her. At first, Kourtney is guarded and quiet. After a while, a cheery, don't-worry-be-happy Kourtney emerges. They have to rein her in without killing that happy spirit. She encourages the others. Everybody loves this girl. Now, after two years with the Glasers, she has returned to live with her mother. This doesn't sit well with the kids. They miss Kourtney and are both angry and sad at the loss. But they're used to feeling this way, so they just go on.

Soon after Kourtney leaves, James, Rachel, Michelle, and Jacob are playing Uno at a game table, and I decide to butt in. I notice the table is of inlaid wood. I'm glad someone donated this table. They let me sit there with them. They slap cards onto the table, in turn. Jacob is winning. They start to talk.

"People use us as a stopping point in their lives," Rachel says. "Then they leave. Look at Sticks. When things got good for him, he left. Kourtney was here when things were bad for her, and then when things got good, she went back to her mom."

James gets his back up and counters, "That's not true. It's not her fault her momma came to get her."

"I don't want Sticks to come back unless he means it," Michelle says quietly, and everyone nods in agreement.

I suggest that Sticks may be hesitant to come back because everyone is mad at him for falling off the wagon and then leaving. There's a serious silence. They are surprised I said that. Of *course* they aren't mad at him, they all say. People going in and out of their lives is just the way things go. People get on the wagon and fall off the wagon. But they still want Sticks to mean it if he comes back.

As Jessie thinks of Kourtney, she says the leave-taking of children is part of the job. Four foster children have come and gone from her home this year. "As a ministry, we accept it. On a personal level, it's hard. I lost a daughter, but I'm happy she got to the point she was able to go back to her mother."

***

Like the Glasers, Jim and Debbie take in foster children and bring other kids to Neighborhood Academy because, Jim says, "Government programs have too many side effects."

While Aid to Dependent Families at one time paid women to not have a father in the home, Welfare-to-Work now takes mothers out of the home. In this neighborhood, the mothers aren't going to jobs that allow for family togetherness. Downtown women working in gas stations and factories don't even consider telling their bosses they'll be late because they have to get the kids off to school. They just go to work and let the system figure out what to do with their kids. "In the end," Jim says, "you have people like Jessie taking in more children because there are no parents at home in the mornings."

In 2005, before his adoption by Jim and Debbie Strietelmeier, it was difficult for Jacob to muster a smile. This photo was taken that year, shortly after he and his sister, Michelle, were sent to live at the Marion County Children's Home.

7

The Bus Ride

It's a relatively new white bus with Neighborhood Fellowship's name emblazoned on the side. On a sunny October day in 2005 Jim steps into the driver's seat. Today's passengers, siblings Johnny, Kelly and Hope, plus John, Justin, Kim, Michelle and Jacob, shuffle to their seats. Justin and Kim are taking home bags of bread someone had donated to the school.

Jim banters with the kids while keeping order. John isn't talking nice.

"John, you're done talking," Jim says.

The offended parties tell John he has to say he's sorry. He complies, and once again, he's their big Teddy bear pal. In laughter and kidlike jostling, someone swats him on the head with a baseball cap, John swipes back, and all is well. In Christian fashion, forgiveness is granted. Jacob and Hope have already forgotten and are starting a stare-down contest in the back seat.

The first stop is Kim's house. It sits in a pocket of niceness, in a row of prim bungalows. There are newly planted petunias in the front garden. Jim waits until she is inside before he moves on.

The bus goes up and down city streets, bumping and banging through alleys, past the Outlaws gang headquarters and other unkempt properties. Every now and then, there's a house with flowers and actual porch furniture out front instead of a cast-off couch or washing machine. The kids get off at various stops, some of them before houses most of us wouldn't want to call home. During this ride, the kids veer away from the calm order of the Academy toward the uncertainty of home. Hope and Kelly help Johnny as they plod toward their house, dawdling as if to stay outside just a few more minutes.

At his stop, Justin is greeted by a yard of weedy stubble and a forbidding, dark house. Brown sheets hanging inside the windows shut out the sunlight. I can only imagine the gloom shut up inside that house. Justin bravely lopes off the bus and hops onto the front porch.

Michelle and Jacob are the last ones on the bus, which is now headed for the Marion County Children's Home where the two siblings live.

"Why can't we go home with you?" Jacob pleads. Jim tells him it's up to the caseworker.

"I hope my mother stops cussing," Michelle says, downcast.

"Me too," Jacob chimes in. "She gets really mad. Can we come and live with you?"

Jim tells them he has visited their mother. He has also spoken with their caseworker.

A solemn silence hangs in the back of the bus.

"Was my mom crying that she missed us?" asks Michelle.

Jacob asks, "Why can't we come and live with you?

Jim replies, "The caseworker will have to look at our house."

Jacob says, "I know. Can you pick us up Sunday?"

Jim says, "If we can, I will. It's not enough for us to want you, Jacob. We do. But as I said, it's up to the caseworker."

Long silence.

Michelle, brightening, says, "One of the girls is going to French braid my hair tonight, and I can't wait. It's gonna hurt, but I know I can take the pain."

At the Children's Home, a woman at the desk checks Michelle and Jacob in. They wave as she walks them away, looking back at Jim until a door closes and they are gone.

***

"What went wrong here?" I ask. One problem was Michelle's and Jacob's living conditions, which Jim described politely as their mother not keeping the house clean. But, he adds, "At some point, unwilling becomes unable."

Eight people live in their house, and all but Jacob and Michelle are mentally and physically disabled.

Having two more under their own roof would be nothing new to the Strietelmeiers.

"We had eight years of my mother and grandmother living with us. There were four generations in our house," Jim says, cheerfully. "We had a guy living in the garage, but the cocaine use was cause for eviction. The basement's still available."

Debbie's parents have lived with them, too. More recently, Eric and Kate Scott, their first baby, and Kristy Alsmeyer all lived in the Strietelmeier home.

Adding two more children to their own four may be routine in numbers, but emotionally, financially, and physically, it will likely be less than a picnic. But here's the motivation: Jim remembers a student named Anna who was removed from her home after being raped by her mother's boyfriend. Child welfare shuffled papers, and Anna, until she was lost to the Strietelmeiers and Neighborhood Academy. They never heard from her, or about her, again. They don't want the system to likewise swallow Michelle and Jacob.

***

One May day in 2008 I'm once again riding the bus with Michelle and Jacob, who are now Michelle and Jacob Strietelmeier. I recall the bus ride a year ago when Jacob and Michelle so forlornly asked Jim if they could come and live with him and Debbie. The adoption was finalized by the end of 2007. James and his sister Jamesha are in the back, and Jamesha is bouncing a ball. Moses Strietelmeier is in a middle seat, and Kimberly is looking out a window. There's a box of bread on the front seat, and Jim tells Jamesha, "Take that box of bread and give it to the neighbors."

"We ain't got no neighbors," James says.

Jim replies, "Go find some."

A kid is outside the bus riding a scooter, and Jacob wants to know if you could be arrested for riding a scooter on the sidewalk. He is concerned about things like this.

Michelle keeps order as Jim stops to buy gas for $3.99 a gallon at the local Speedway station. Someone is swinging from a bar in the front of the bus next to the driver's seat, and Michelle tells him to stop it. Jim gets back on the bus, saying he just bought ten gallons of gas for $40. It used to cost $50 to fill the whole tank, Jim said.

On the way to drop off Kimberly, we pass the house where seven members of a family were murdered last year.

Kimberly, who is being adopted by Mike and Cindy Hayes, is by now teasing Jacob. She gets off the bus at the Hayes home. Jim says a man named Bill lives across the street and points to the house. Bill sometimes howls at the moon.

The bus goes back over to Beville to park in front of the Strietelmeier home. This, instead of the Marion County Children's Home, is now Michelle and Jacob's stop. Jim parks the bus, and we all get off.

Inside, we chat around the kitchen table, and Debbie brings a bowl of dill green beans, straight from the can. "You just have to try these," she says, explaining that Roger Graham—the man who carts furniture to the church from the suburbs—has brought a case of them over and someone has to eat them. It might as well be me. Besides, these beans are really good, and so I ask for a second helping.

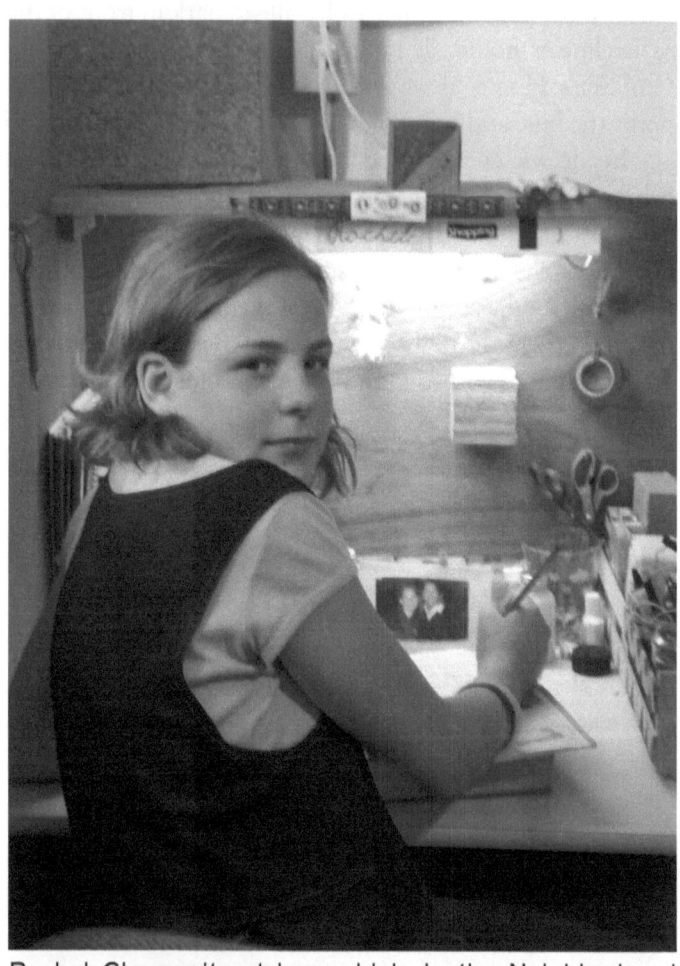

Rachel Glaser sits at her cubicle in the Neighborhood Academy classroom in 2005. Like the Strietelmeiers, the Glasers live and minister in the inner city.

8

The Rules Rule

[1]You shall have no other gods before me.

[2]You shall not make for yourself an idol.

[3]You shall not make wrongful use of the name of the Lord your God.

[4]Remember the Sabbath day, and keep it holy.

[5]Honor your father and your mother, so that your days may be long in the land that the Lord your God is giving you.

[6]You shall not murder.

[7]You shall not commit adultery.

[8]You shall not steal.

[9]You shall not bear false witness against your neighbor.

[10]You shall not covet anything that belongs to your neighbor.

—*The Ten Commandments*

The inner city boasts some pretty strange rules to live by. For starters, taking your cultural rules of the suburbs to the corridor of East Tenth Street is like hauling your living room couch with you to the beach. The couch works fine in the living room but looks ridiculous and doesn't work too well around sand, wind and water. Likewise, if you come to live downtown and haul the rules of societal politeness along, they will be more than useless. There's a strong likelihood that politeness will make you a victim.

The idea is not to be rude, but to realize that what works in small-town America—the politeness of unlocked doors, tact so as not to hurt anyone's feelings, smiling at strangers—will likely get you robbed in the inner city.

The general rule on the street is, get what you can, however you can get it. Getting it requires obedience to a maze of sub-rules.

According to Jim Strietelmeier, if a guy asks you for a dollar, *and you don't want to give it to him*, you can't tactfully lie that you don't have a dollar. That's being polite—not saying what you're really thinking. That kind of politeness breaks the urban sub-rule of entitlement: what's yours is mine, stranger, and if you mess with me (lie to me), I'll just take what you have.

The next thing you know, you've been mugged. Thieves know you have that dollar, and they don't respect the lie.

The rule is to tell the guy *why* you're not giving him the dollar. When Jim doesn't want to give up the dollar, he tells the beggar, "I don't know you."

That way, the guy knows he's the one breaking the rules because there you are, two people standing there as strangers. The rules say that if the beggar and you are strangers, he's entitled to what you have so he should have just mugged you in the first place. By street rules, a person must know a specific individual before *asking* him for money.

Urban beggars knowingly break this rule when they commute to the suburbs to stand at the busy intersection waiting to buttonhole drivers caught at stoplights. You've seen these guys. They hold signs announcing different versions of the same old sob story: "Homeless. Will work for food," or "Disabled vet, need help," or "Disabled vet, four kids, hungry."

Jim's advice, whether you give or don't give to panhandlers, is to make your choice without apology. He says it's a mistake in this neighborhood to show empty hands as though you are sorry, but you have no money. Since the beggar is asking you, a stranger, for money there is no obligation for you to (a) politely lie or (b) hand over money. The beggar knows this rule but thinks you don't. He knows polite people feel guilty, and like a child trying to wheedle unearned cash from a parent, he thinks you'll give in.

If you truly want to give cash to this stoplight beggar or hand him that burger you just bought at the drive-through, by all means give it to him. After all, God loves a cheerful giver. If you don't want to, drive away without guilt. That's the rule, according to Jim.

On a daily basis, people ask Jim for food or clothing, and the earnest are not turned away. In giving them what they need physically, he tells them, "Either you've walked away from God and He's calling you back by your need or you're like Job, in the midst of God declaring His glory. Either way, you need to call upon His name."

He's found that people respond to this.

"It's that brutal honesty, that loving honesty, that I'm really good at," Jim said. "I can look affluent folks in the eye and say, 'Don't waste your life with all this cash.' I can look a poor person in the eye and say. 'I love you. Don't waste your life on all this idleness.'"

***

Another urban rule is to accept that your possessions are always being eyed by someone else. This would be coveting as in commandment ten. Believers in the Ten Commandments want to live up to this rule. Downtown, it's a good thing the Strietelmeiers, the Glasers and the others consider their possessions temporary and not their own. From the stolen roosters to cell phones and the church's stained glass window, another robbery is just another robbery. They sigh and call the police, though the police just snickered when a neighbor reported the stolen roosters in the early spring of 2008.

Jim and Deb can't keep a lawn mower through the summer. Twice a year, mowers are taken from their garage. When the mower goes missing, Jim goes to the lawn mower store to see if it's shown up there. Once, he had to buy back his own mower. When Jim went looking after the last theft, the man at the shop told him, "Oh, I saw your mower. Someone was pushing it down the street."

The Strietelmeiers' van has been broken into, stolen, and shot at. The bullet hole in the side tells the story of how it was probably the get-away van for a robbery or used in a drive-by shooting.

Just as people judge Jim by his address (they say, "Oh. I'm sorry to hear that.") and by the beat-up van (they mostly just look away), he says his real personhood is not in his address or in what he drives. He said it's not even in the way he looks, now that a dentist has pulled a baby tooth that hung on to his lower jaw until well after Jim's forty-second birthday. He thinks he now has a gap-tooth smile, but I frankly don't see any difference, because you can't see people's lower teeth when they smile. The face of someone who cares day in and day out for widows and orphans is beautiful with or without a snaggletooth.

"I now look a little more like one of the homeless," he

jokes about the missing tooth. "While these flaws are not who I am, they certainly represent me. I choose to live where I live, I choose to drive what I drive because we need a fifteen-passenger van, and my teeth help me identify with the poor." Still, he points out, dentist Dr. Gary Walton "looks after me and my family."

***

The Ten Commandments are rules God gave to all of us. They may in some ways translate differently, depending on who you are and where you are situated, but in the end, they're the same for everyone. The above rules might be confusing. God's rules are not—until people complicate them with their own interpretations, depending on their culture or political point of view.[1]

The most-quoted of God's Ten Commandments is, "Thou shalt not kill." The word Moses saw struck on the tablet by God's own hand was the Hebrew word for murder. Though the command, "Thou shalt not kill" is pretty cut-and-dry, Jim has noticed a contrast in how urban and rural cultures view murder.

"I've known Joe since he was six. He gets really religious when he's in trouble," Jim says. "He was in real trouble when he killed a man on Tenth Street during a fistfight. Both the men were so drunk they couldn't protect themselves, but Joe was young and strong enough to land the last punch. The guy he killed fell backward, hit his head on the curb, and died three days later. Joe was convicted of involuntary manslaughter and ended up spending four months in jail.

"Here's an irony: rob a bank, and you're not coming out until you're gray. Joe got four months for killing another man. Money has more value than life. I know a number of

---

1 See the Appendix for Jim's contrasts of all Ten Commandments between urban and suburban cultures.

murderers, but I don't know any bank robbers. They're all in jail.

"Murder is cheap here. It's become a crime that, unless it's spectacular, is pretty much winked at. That's a city problem. Suburban areas address murder in the old way. They think it's serious."

The Strietelmeiers gather for lunch around their dining room table at home, which is opened to dozens of people who share meals at any given time. Minus Moses and Jacob, they are (from left) Jim, Michelle, Elizabeth, Debbie, Joseph and Abigail.

9

The Wealth of Having Nothing

In Neighborhood Fellowship's first 10 years, the Strietelmeiers gave away about 80 cars, in addition to watches, clothes, food and furniture that passed through their hands on the way to others. People just give them stuff. Jim has also acquired a couple of houses, three church buildings and a few other structures around town. Some were donated, others bought cheap.

Jim and Debbie stopped counting the number of cars they'd given away six years ago, when the count was fifty. Here's how it works: Jim casually lets someone know a mother with four kids needs a car. It gets put in a church bulletin somewhere, and sure enough, along comes someone who realizes he really doesn't *need* to sell that old car of his for a few hundred bucks. He gives it to Jim.

A watch given to Jim will end up on someone else's wrist. The Thanksgiving turkey you took down to their home won't be sitting on their table. Someone else will need those nice shoes, the clothes, the money you give to the Strietelmeiers.

Church buildings pass through his hands like water through a sieve. "I collect churches," Jim says, brightly.

He will be sitting there one day trying to figure out who pinched his guitar or cell phone, and someone will call to say there's an old country church this congregation doesn't want any more. Does he want it? Sure. Then he's likely to give it away.

Jim has the mind-set of the evangelist who once announced to his audience, "We're all renters, here, because it all belongs to God anyway. Eventually, someone else will be living in your house or driving your car or wearing your clothes."

Along these same lines, the Strietelmeiers would really rather be in Africa, so they consider themselves "momentary fixtures" at the Neighborhood Fellowship building. It, too, was someone else's before it became the home of their congregation. But it was always God's. They acquired it in the early days of Neighborhood Fellowship, when their living room began to overcrowded. Jim found the big, ancient church building for sale just a few blocks away. He asked his wealthy friends for guidance in this matter, and people from Zionsville Fellowship funded the purchase.

"Ask for advice and people will give you money," Jim says. "Ask people for money, and they will give you advice."

Others would come alongside, struggling with Jim to fix up the seemingly hopeless old structure. It's been a long haul, and for all the work, parts of the building are still in disrepair. But most of it has blossomed under the care of loving hands.

Still, Jim and Deb are more concerned with souls than with brick and mortar. "If I need a perfect building, I'm in trouble," Jim says. "We would have to do fundraising, and none of us have the time for that."

So, they bear the trouble of an old building because they have low expectations for bling and fluff.

"When you are ministering to the poor, it's not a 'get-ahead' plan," Jim says.

It wasn't long before Jim heard about an empty church building in his old neighborhood, near Broad Ripple. Next thing you know, the people who owned the church said, "Here, Jim, you take it." The next thing after that, Jim and Phil were teaching there on Sunday mornings before returning to Neighborhood Fellowship's afternoon service. The church became spin-off of Neighborhood Fellowship. They called this one Olive Branch Fellowship.

Another church came his way, this one to the north in the Clinton County countryside near Sheridan. The original owners of the land had left it to their church with the stipulation the property would always be used as for church purposes. The church was built, a century passed, and the structure aged along with its members. Those left in congregation by the twenty-first century gave the land and hundred-year-old building to Jim, with the original conditions attached. Jim let a Reformed Presbyterian group use the building for the cost of insurance, but the Lord had other plans. Lightning struck, and it burned to the ground, except for the foundation and the foyer.

The insurance money enabled the Presbyterians to find their own place to rent. Jim's dream is to have a retreat camp on the old church grounds for the people—especially the kids—of Neighborhood Fellowship. But that's another story.

In 2008, he got a call about an old warehouse in Indianapolis that was for sale ... cheap that could be a great school.

The Strietelmeiers don't apologize for expecting the

wealthy to give. To them, that's the way things are supposed to be in the Christian world.

"We try to avoid the direct ask," Jim says. "I value those who are affluent, but I don't value them for their money. God is the resource. He motivates people to give. I tell a crowd about a need, but I want individual relationships to be free of the stress money brings."

Much is expected of those to whom monetary wealth is given. He says American Christianity is in pathetic shape, because of its trust in fiscal prosperity. When it comes to caring for the needy, for orphans and widows and providing for the stranger in the land and doing good to all men, as the Bible instructs, "Christians try at it, but we wouldn't have a welfare system if they were good at it," Jim says. "The church has an inadequate plan because right now it has an inadequate view of heaven. The Bible describes heaven like this: the sufferings of this life are not worthy to be compared to the glories to come."

***

As for his view of material wealth, Jim says he has learned much about people's sense of entitlement, or thinking that their work created their wealth. After all, did God not give these folks the ability—not to mention the breath—to work?

All classes of people feel entitlement at some level, he explains. "If you're born into a rich family, you feel entitled. If you're rich because you were born into a working family, and you went to college, you think, 'I deserve wealth.'"

But think about this, then: the poor person was born into the poor family who didn't feed him right or educate him right. Did he then deserve the poverty that follows? The American psyche says yes, they do deserve their lot because they made poor choices.

"I don't have a gripe with wealth or poverty," Jim says. "Generally, neither is always deserved. Some deserve poverty because they are fools. Then, there are poor people who have worked hard who deserve blessing, too. There are wealthy who have done little on their own, by way of earning that wealth. We can't encourage the thinking that says, 'I deserve my place.' The truth is, we deserve God's judgment all the time."

***

The aim for the children at Neighborhood Academy is not escape. It is to give them hope through faith in Jesus Christ as their redeemer; to educate them with knowledge and compassion so that one day they will return to help another generation. This, then, is a story of triumph over tragedy; of relentless refusal to give in to what skeptics and demographers like to call "overwhelming odds."

To give an idea of the odds in those early days, Jim wrote this to one of the churches supporting the downtown effort: "Our greatest struggle this year has been dealing with an informal, unorganized, dangerous, needy, irresponsible culture while being closely tied to an organized, relatively self-sufficient, responsible culture. Living where we do has made for a hectic life rather than a particularly fruitful one."

In the midst of all of this, two cultures come together. Volunteers ebb and flow like faithful, orderly tides. People come down to serve the free meals offered after services on Sundays. They take up hammers and nails and paint brushes. At the school, volunteers have the grueling task of teaching children who have little interest in reading to read. They are the faithful who help make possible a gleaming hope for people who are largely ignored.

There are volunteers who come with motives of true

concern, who fumble and sometimes say the wrong things, but their hearts are right. Like a healthy tide, their presence floods nourishment in and washes the dead wood out. Then, there are others who roll sluggishly in—stagnant tides—curious observers rather than helpers. But the Strietelmeiers, the Glasers, the Hales, and the Jacksons gratefully welcome them all. They welcomed me, too.

I remember the first time I went down with a group to serve the Sunday meal. I was a stagnant tide. I didn't want to eat the food. It was chicken on white bread—the Neighborhood Fellowship version of chicken a-la-king. Boy, I felt really good about myself, though. Here I was *helping the needy*. Every spoonful of chicken a-la-king slung onto a paper plate was a jewel in my crown. Oh, how they must have appreciated *me*. I nodded and smiled at people, proud of my own largesse at giving up a Sunday afternoon to come here. God would love me more for this. The Strietelmeiers, Glasers, and Jacksons hugged me and hung out with me. If they then went home and prayed for me, God answered their prayers, but it took nearly a year.

Even as a committed Christian, in that effort I was shameful, prideful, haughty, and all of those words for things God hates. The truth of my motives began to dawn on me, but I grasped at a loophole. Well, at least I went down there, I told myself. I mean, after all, some people would never set foot in that neighborhood. I had just added smug to the list to the things I was. God wasn't going to let me do that. He nipped at my heels, hounding me to get real, to shed this awful shell. To go back there and learn. I fought. I had things to do. I had a job. The Lord got rid of my job.

Okay, okay, I'll go. I won't be smug. I'll be humble. That's it, I'll be humble. I went, and I was so very humbly smug. This time, I even sat with some people and ate some Jell-O. See? I was humble.

The hound of heaven came back, fierce.

Okay, okay. I went back and took an official reporter's notebook along, proud to announce I was a writer. I would tell the world about Jim and Deb Strietelmeiers' good work. They were very kind about all of my grandiose plans. But things didn't go so well with my story. I couldn't get it right. I prayed, I begged the Lord for His words, but they were all mine, and nothing sounded real. It was hollow and shallow, and I knew it. When was God going to help me? Was this really His work or mine?

Months went by, and I didn't feel so proud any more. I realized I didn't know so much after all. I was still just on the surface as far as Neighborhood Fellowship was concerned. It was a duty, not a love. Not that I was actually humble. These things take time. But during that time, I met kids who were braver and smarter than I ever hoped to be, kids who persevered under unbelievable stress. I met adults who really loved them and who also persevered and overcame. Who weren't self-serving but were about serving others.

In spite of my slowness of heart, I went weekly to the school. A scale or two of this shell of resistance I seemed to have fell off each time. Suddenly, it wasn't about a book. In fact, the book fell by the wayside for a season. Instead, I fell in love, not with my own vision, but with the people and the children. With the Lord's mercy, more scales fell. The old building became my friend, greeting me each time I arrived. I'd look for its bell tower as I approached and feel at home. Everything would be okay now, because here were all of the dear, faithful people—the real church. Here was comfort. God allowed me to feel a tiny bit of what the kids feel when they see that steeple tower and enter those doors. But at the end of the day, I went home to affluence, while they went home to troubles.

There came a time I thought I should stop observing,

interviewing, and taking notes and start being involved. Maybe I could man the chair or something. I didn't feel, really, that I had much to offer. Funny thing, when I mentioned this to Jessie, she told me there was a girl who needed tutoring in English so that she could graduate.

Actually, we both graduated that year. Crystal from high school, and me from ignorance.

***

Some nice ladies once came to the Strietelmeier home to teach summertime Vacation Bible School for kids in the neighborhood. They had that polite look the Strietelmeirs have come to know as the one that says, "I love you but, um, am I really safe here?"

One of the women went beyond the look. As she headed to the kitchen for a glass of tap water, she paused to ask Deb, "Is the water here okay to drink?"

Dearest lady, we're all on the same water. The water supply of most Indianapolis suburbs comes from the Indianapolis Water Company. The Indianapolis Water Company also serves Beville Street.

***

Two women wanted to plant flowers in front of the church. You know the unspoken reasoning: if these poor people could look at some flowers and see this property spruced up a little bit, they'd feel better.

The ladies thought they would demonstrate how perky the 'hood would look with a few pretty flowers.

Jim told the women the truth: please don't come and do that, because the flowers will be vandalized. But the women were on a mission. They came anyway, toting a flat of hardy petunias, and went to work in the patch of rock-hard clay, which no one had cultivated in more than half a century.

After they left, Sticks was out there admiring the flower bed when he found a set of keys that had been dropped.

Sure enough, one of the women called to claim the keys. She asked Jim if he would mind bringing them to her husband's place of work at a prestigious address in downtown Indy. She gave him a time that would be convenient.

Of course, said Jim.

He was ready to hang up and happily make the drive when the woman added a needless disclaimer: "After all, my husband drives a BMW, and we don't think it would be wise for him to drive in your neighborhood."

Now, it is true that taking an old car downtown and leaving the Beemer at home is something you should just do. *Quietly.* The woman might as well have told Jim she didn't want to wear her Saks slacks to Neighborhood Fellowship because she might have to sit on the furniture.

Still, he'd made a commitment, so Jim got into the old, enormous blue van and drove to the husband's office building. When he pulled up to a curb in the parking lot, a security guard told him he couldn't park there. He explained he was dashing in to leave a set of keys. He held up a brown paper bag containing the keys. The guard said, "Okay, but park over there," pointing to an out-of-the-way spot, away from the Beemers and Lexii. "And be quick about it."

Maybe these folks shouldn't drive expensive cars in Jim's neighborhood, but it was clear it also wasn't cool to drive an old van to this place. Feeling like he'd been profiled as the Unabomber, Jim parked and walked through metal detectors to arrive at the front desk at the appointed time.

"You can't leave that here," the woman at the desk said sternly, pointing to Jim's paper bag. He opened it to prove it only contained keys and not a bomb. She agreed to call the husband's office and then sent an e-mail, announcing Jim's arrival with *the Package*. He had to stay with *the Package*.

Minutes passed. No answer. She left Jim's cell phone number on voicemail and sent a second e-mail. Minutes dragged on, painfully. Five. Ten. Fourteen. Jim stood there, holding the offending paper bag, hoping he looked innocent and pleasant.

In strode the guard, hitching up his belt the way cops do when they want to register authority. He told the clerk that he was there "to make sure everything's normal." He gave Jim the visual once-over and hovered until Jim gave up and returned with the paper bag to his car. He was driving away when the husband rang his cell phone to say he'd be right out to get the keys. Jim pulled the van back onto the prestigious property and waited, the guard eyeing him suspiciously. The husband came out of the building and Jim smiled and handed him the bag with the keys.

"Well," said the smiling husband, "I'm glad we could connect, Jim. And wow, that's quite a place you have there, from what my wife says. She loved coming down to help, *but, well, heh, heh, she's really a neatness freak.*"

Jim laughed along and drove off, pondering the backhanded remark. The man probably didn't realize the unspoken gist of what he had said: "Your property is dirty."

Some people who come down to help really don't realize they are difficult to work with. "They think *we're* the problem," Jim says, laughing.

The flowers were uprooted within the week. That was after the van was stolen and returned with a bullet hole in the side. In July and August that same summer of 2006, police were called nine times.

So, bring an old car downtown, if you can get your hands on one. But do it quietly. No announcement necessary.

Fred Anderson followed his dream and opened the Clean America Laundromat next door to the Rivoli Theatre. There, he sat with people, listened to their sad stories and shared in their joys. He borrowed from the Neighborhood Fellowship clothing closet to sell clothes for a buck to those in need.

10

Hardly the End

Fred Anderson had a dream one night. He dreamed he owned a Laundromat, of all things. In fact, his was the biggest Laundromat in America.

Fred used to be the human resources director for the Chicago accounting firm, Arthur Anderson & Co. He now has Parkinson's disease. The Laundromat dream nagged at him.

"Fred has God-size dreams," Jim commented.

Fred puzzled over his dream, mulled it over, and shrugged, figuring God would show him if this was a vision or a silly playing of the brain in the middle of the night. As he pulled up in front of Neighborhood Fellowship one day, he noticed for the first time the building across the street.

An old sign on the obviously neglected building said, "A to Z Laundromat."

As he stared at the sign, Fred envisioned the once-thriving neighborhood, with busy people in the 1940s and '50s carrying basketfuls of laundry in and out of the A to Z. He imagined it had once been a hub of talk and camaraderie for housewives. Like the rest of the neighborhood, it had long-ago shed decent-looking paint, appealing signage, and any greenery that might have grown in the space between sidewalk and building.

No one was inside, save for a jobless man looking for warmth. The old washers and dryers sat motionless. No one could afford the four quarters that bought a washerload of clean clothes.

That was enough for Fred. He found the owner and arranged for a lease-purchase agreement on the building. The A to Z sign was the first thing to go. In its place, a banner announced that the Laundromat was now named Clean America. It was like a book title, because a subheading reads, "From Sea to Shining Sea," just like in Fred's dream. Above the sign he placed a new American flag.

Fred struggled with a shovel and dirt busters to plant a row of flowers next to the building, despite warnings they could be uprooted by people who wanted them for their own yards.

But he soldiered on with his little garden, painstakingly forcing the tools in his tremoring hands to do what he wanted them to do.

When I walk over to the Clean America Laundromat for a talk one day, he takes me inside the building, bringing the tools inside, too. Anyone who would steal flowers would have no qualms about hauling off with Fred's trowel.

Inside, he shows me the racks of clothes from the Neighborhood Fellowship closet, which he sells for $1. People appreciate and are proud of something they buy, he says.

"I originally wanted to find a building in a high-end locale," he says. "But when I got here, I knew this was it. My vision is for relationships. That's our work and our future."

A row of chairs is where Fred has comforted many a customer. He introduces them to Jesus Christ.

Fred was the sower in the neighborhood for a few years, and then the Parkinson's took over and the Laundromat went under. There's a for-sale sign in the window that has not gone unnoticed by Jim. Meanwhile, the American flag, now miserably tattered, forlornly flaps its shredded stripes in the winter wind of 2010. Someone really ought to take that flag down. Note: Someone finally did, as of May 13, 2010.

***

Things are looking physically better at Tenth and Rural.

Indianapolis Public School No. 54, Brookside Elementary, new and shining, now stands behind and wraps to the east of Neighborhood Fellowship. The school district, which once threatened an eminent domain takeover of Neighborhood Fellowship, never touched that property.

The church has a new sign, and someone has planted a few trees out front. Flowers bloom now out front where Sticks's dog, T-2, is buried. Just last week, some kids from Covenant Christian School came and planted some more flowers and added mulch. Yes, people are still planting flowers and people are still uprooting them. But it sure looks nice for a while. Maybe this summer things will be different.

If Neighborhood Fellowship and its Academy were merely a Hollywood movie, little Johnny, the boy with cerebral palsy, would find a benefactor who would use money and a change of scenery to ease his life. Jofus might have played the role of a dropout who came back to school and eventually became a famous writer or theologian. Gabby, Kim, and Crystal would soar to the heights after college and become lawyers or doctors or schoolteachers back in the inner city to lift the others up. Big John would overcome his own sorrows and find joy in life. Maybe Michelle and Jacob would be adopted by Jim and Deb, and Jacob would miraculously become a joyful kid. Perhaps Kourtney and James and Rachel and Mimi, Bethany, and the others would likewise make good.

In Hollywood, Sticks would probably continue mopping and serving lunches, inspiring the kids and adults at the school. Jim and Deb would go off to Africa. Barry and Jessie would adopt some of their foster kids so the children wouldn't have the pain of being wrenched away.

But God, not Hollywood, scripted the story here. The last scene for Neighborhood Fellowship is far from written, but this book must come to its last page sometime. And so I will tell how things stand as the last page approaches. It's spring of 2009.

Sticks completed cancer treatments and went back to drinking. Neighborhood Fellowship sent him to a Christ-centered, twelve-month residential recovery program called Hebron, run by Wheeler Mission. In the process, counselors discovered that Charles Steven "Sticks" Riggle had gotten his nickname from gang members, in honor of his chosen weapon for punishment of others. The counselors put the kibosh on that name, and his past, by thereafter referring to him as Charles. It is the hope that his given name will give him a new view of himself.

After seven weeks in the program, Charles did what so many addicts do, and said to himself, "I'm okay now," and left. That was the beginning of another long absence from Neighborhood Fellowship and long days and nights of drunken stupor. By May 2008, he was still glaringly absent from the church, and the kids were still disappointed.

Jim, Barry, and Phil told Charles, "If you come back, we're going to love you enough to send you back to Camp Hunt (where the Wheeler Mission program is administered, near Bloomington, Indiana)." That's just what happened in the summer of 2008. As I write, Sticks is once again walking in the way of a Christian.

By the time of his father's death on February 13, 2009, Sticks had been Charles for some time. As his father lay dying after a serious fall, Charles sat at his bedside reading Scripture and praying. He washed his father's feet. Upon hearing this, I recall the tattoo, "Dad the Best."

"He was the only one there that night, with his father," Jim said. "And for the first time in his Charles-life, he knew his dad was proud of him."

In spring of 2009, I once again talk with Charles (I call him Stic—Charles). He is living next door to the Strietelmeiers, now. He has severed part of his index finger in a wood chipper. "Now I don't have a pointin' finger," he says, laughing. "I'll just have to give people the look and the point. Don't make me slam my hand down on the table, either."

He says that, in spite of his new identity, he still wants to have "Sticks" added to his birth certificate as part of his legal name. I don't know what that means in the larger scheme of recovery, but I nod and say "Well, okay, Charles."

He is proud of going through the Hebron recovery program at Camp Hunt. He says he is going back to Neighborhood Fellowship ("I get over to the church now and then."). Charles tells Jim he is continuing with the Lord and his sobriety. They all expect the Lunch Lady to be back, soon.

"He's a changed man," Jim now says. "God did such a work in him."

Jim, Deb, Abigail, Elizabeth, Moses, and Joseph adopted Michelle and Jacob, but nothing about it was Hollywood. Jacob's deep-seated anger was taking him headlong down the road of disaster as he beat up on Moses, stole things from the family, and caused agonizing disruption in the family. The whole community continued to pray for Jacob.

As God would have it, Jacob changed one day in October of 2007. Jim was correcting him on the porch, for the umpteenth time, about the same behavior problems: Slapping Moses around. Fighting about bedtime. Fighting his way through meals. Cranking up the belligerence when it was time to do chores. Resentment had percolated in his vulnerable young mind for years, and Jacob was just plain sullen and mad. Nothing was helping. Jim and Deb were at the end of their rope, and so the Lord took over.

Jim expected Jacob to argue there on the front porch. He didn't. Then and there, his demeanor changed. His countenance changed. Jacob was actually sorry. No, not sorry. That's a word for merely feeling bad about making poor decisions. Jacob was repentant. His heart, in an instant, changed.

"He didn't suddenly become a good child," Jim said. "He moved from being a dangerous child to just a difficult one. It was the work of God. He went to bed that night without a fight. The next day, he did his chores, smiling, helpful, and full of joy. He's on his way to good."

Deb said Jacob "became a good child," in that his attitude changed, but not some of his ingrained bad habits. They are dealing with those, she said, "But the difference is, he loves us now."

The next time I saw Jacob was at the adoption ceremony in late 2007. Gone was the long face. His eyes were different—no longer blank. I saw that his God-given change was not a demonstration of temporary remorse or some manipulative performance. No, Jacob really changed.

Just before Jim took Jacob to a church men's retreat in 2008, "He made the next step from difficult to being pleasant," Jim said.

At school, after that, Jacob actually looked at me for the first time. I recalled his former vacant face, which would have been a poker player's envy.

When Jacob asked on the bus that long-ago day if he and Michelle could go home with Jim instead of back to the Marion County children's home, it was in a monotone, as though he was resigned to being miserable, no matter what the answer. He was there but not there at the same time, whether at school or on the bus or on the playground.

By spring 2010, the goodness is still there. He and Moses study side by side, joshing as teenage brothers will do. I see two young men with promising futures.

Michelle is a beautiful young woman. She always remembers the earrings I sneaked to her during the adoption ceremony, where we were asked not to bring gifts. I couldn't help it, Jim and Deb. I couldn't picture those earrings on anyone else's ears but Michelle's. Her eyes have changed, too. She no longer looks scared. She's quieter. She's no longer frantically looking for acceptance because she's learned that she is loved.

Abigail, ever-studious and ever-playing in the church band, plans to attend Moody Bible Institute in 2011, while Elizabeth, with a mind of her own set on social justice, continues her high school studies with a new, teenagerly streak of red in her hair. Moses now sports braces on his teeth and and plows through his work with a penchant for writing articles in the school newsletter. Joseph has joined the classroom now and likes to keep his coat on while studying. One word describes Joseph: chipper.

John lost a ton of weight and gained confidence onstage in Aaron Alsmeyer's musical. He found further success on a city basketball team.

In the neighborhood, as is the case everywhere, the economic climate has changed to the point that even the homeless are being robbed. Everyone's sneakers are once again subject to theft. But it's not only sneakers. Last spring, a man described by neighbors as portly and carrying a flapping yellow sack made off with two roosters from the Strietelmeiers' backyard. And just last November, Jim and Deb shouted yet another a burglar out of their home, having no other weapon but their voices.

***

The Alsmeyer and Walsman families have merged. If you can follow this, here's how it went: Aaron Alsmeyer and Beth Walsman got married and moved into the other half of a double bought by Beth and her brother, Joel. Joel Walsman married Aaron's sister, Kristy Alsmeyer, and so all of the brothers and sisters shared the double, eight doors down from the Strietelmeiers. The Walsmans have moved to a bigger home in the neighborhood with their two little ones, and the Alsmeyers just bought a house across the street. Meanwhile, baby Sally Alsmeyer is the most popular kid at Neighborhood Academy as she toddles around, babbling and playing, while Aaron and Beth oversee the classes. The two are expecting a second child. They still attend Zionsville Fellowship, where Aaron plays bass guitar in the worship band.

Aaron's and Kristy's mom, Judy, can still be found in the older kids' classroom a couple of days a week, helping where the Lord needs her.

***

Kim, the girl from the first chapter, with the math story problem and whose father died of the drug overdose, graduated in 2006 from Neighborhood Academy. Like most graduates, she was full of plans. She was bound for a mission trip to Costa Rica in July. After that, she said she'd like to take courses at Crossroads Bible College on Indianapolis' southeast side and then go on to Ivy Tech to study early childhood development.

"I'll see where God leads me from there," she said.

As of this writing, she never went to Costa Rica, but she did take a few classes at Crossroads Bible College in Indianapolis. As of 2009 she lives on the west side of Indianapolis. She has a baby she is raising on her own.

***

Gabby and Crystal graduated in 2007. Gabby had been accepted at Moody Bible Institute in Chicago, and Crystal said she was planning to sign up for classes at Crossroads. Gabby is in her second year studying at Moody. Crystal went back to Broad Ripple to live and was last heard to be working at a fast-food restaurant there while taking classes at Ivy Tech in Indianapolis.

On May 1, 2008, Barry and Jessie adopted Craig, 5, and 7-year-old Timmy and their baby brother, Jason, bringing the total for adoptions with Neighborhood Fellowship connections to nine.

Their daughter Rachel is a pretty teenager who went to the prom with her boyfriend, is a serious student and keeps her younger siblings in line with stern inquiries such as, "Craig, why aren't you at your desk?" She sounds just like her mom, Jessie, of the old days.

***

Justin (Jofus) never came back to school after 2006. He showed up once, feeling like he needed a quick fix of comfort, but other than that, no one has seen him, except for a few times, walking along Michigan Street.

I hear James dropped out of school when he turned 16. Then, the usual happened: like a sailboat loose from its mooring and drifting wherever the cold wind blows, he fell in with some friends most parents would call undesirable.

James, who just two years before shone like a star on the stage, was arrested in 2009 for armed carjacking.

Hope, Kelly, and their brother Johnny—the little guy with cerebral palsy who used to swing in the tire on the playground—moved to Westfield with their mother, Mary, and older sister about the time Jofus left. Westfield is an affluent suburb far to the north of Indianapolis. The week after they moved, Mary—who had suffered a stroke earlier and was receiving disability pay—simply died in her sleep. Johnny found her.

***

What all of these kids have in common is a memory, built at Neighborhood Academy, of a place where they were loved, where people talked about Jesus and healing and being whole. The seeds have been planted, hopefully someday to grow and push through the icy tragedies of their lives and bring restoration to their souls. There is no failure where Christ is concerned.

***

As Aaron and Beth Alsmeyer take over responsibility for the school, dozens continue to help, including Mary Newton, an elderly red-haired lady who comes down on Thursdays to run the library with due librarian strictness and fortitude. Roberta Parks and Gina Streeter lend their reading and teaching expertise every week. Cliff Fiscus teaches history to the high-schoolers. I can't name everyone, but the Lord knows who you are who come down here to make a difference. To earn a living, Aaron works three days a week as a pharmacist. Their perpetually happy baby girl, Sally, comes to school every day and gives the kids a chance to nurture a cute, bald baby.

***

A medical and dental clinic has started at Neighborhood

Fellowship, in cooperation with the Indiana University School of Medicine. Jim says they have an eye on evangelizing the doctors who are donating their time. The clinic opened in spring of 2008, with interns volunteering their time. Six months later, the word was that some 250 medical students had participated.

Neighborhood Fellowship now hosts Mothers' Club, once a ministry of Wheeler Mission. When Wheeler gave up administering Mothers' Club, another local outreach, Shepherd Center, took over. The club meets at Neighborhood Fellowship twice a week. It's taken over the entire second floor, with dozens of mothers showing up on Tuesdays and Thursdays for Bible study, sewing, quilting, GED and computer classes, and other things downtown mothers would not generally be doing. Kim comes with her baby. She looks downcast when I see her on Thursdays, barely able to muster a smile, and I know things are tough for her.

Across town, Olive Branch Church has a Web site, www.urbantime.org. Jim is the video blogger, using each four-minute posting to do things like tell viewers how to get a building. Jim was a subject of Moody Radio's "Today in the Word" show and was featured in the Moody Bible Institute's magazine.

In the meantime, Jim has acquired yet another building—an old pharmacy or apothecary—on the near west side. He also is buying two more homes on his street so that others can live in the Neighborhood as he and Debbie do: To choose poverty for the sake of bringing hope to those who have not chosen to be numbered among the poor.

"None of us has any idea what God is doing here," Jim said. He's just watching and waiting and still longing for Africa.

***

In a final twist of irony, it seems that the poor are drifting to the suburbs. The signs began in the 1950s and '60s, when inner-city student populations began filtering into once upper-middle-class Shortridge and Howe high schools. The schools became blighted with dropouts from homes where the parents were generally AWOL. Along came busing and poverty with all of its ills spread north to formerly affluent Pike and North Central high schools as people moved to be closer to their children's schools, but where they couldn't afford to live. Some struggled honestly and earnestly to fit in. But to this day, there are families who live in cars or do the month-to-month rent but don't pay the rent. These schools now have school police who deal with increasing vandalism, drug dealing and student indifference—or should I say a sense of hopelessness. Where test scores were once the highest in the state, they are now mediocre. The downward spiral is contagious. At elementary schools in Pike and Washington townships, as far north as Eighty-Sixth Street, teachers and aides run interference as kids from all income levels are increasingly swearing, openly fighting and blatantly ignoring homework assignments. One far-northside teachers' aide told me, "We often don't know who the people are who come to parents' night. It could be an aunt, uncle, grandparent, if not a mother's boyfriend or father's girlfriend. That's if anyone bothers to show up at all. Some don't have addresses because they have to move once a month."

Next stop: Carmel and Zionsville.

Meanwhile, upwardly-mobile professional couples are salvaging and renovating cottages and bungalows in the downtown Lockerbie, Woodruff Place and Fountain Square neighborhoods, to name just a few. In 1990, the average cost of a single-family dwelling in Indianapolis was $82,864. By the beginning of 1999, this figure had risen to $125,307, according to Web encyclopedia Advameg's Cities of the World site.

Jim Strietelmeier is only half joking when he tells me he sees a surreal reversal of urban/suburban fortunes in the future: "In a generation or two, Neighborhood Fellowship could be the wealthy church and Zionsville Fellowship will be the poor one, and someone like me will need that building."

If there is a singular, underlying truth that binds what they all are doing in downtown Indianapolis, it is that God is good. "He has promised goodness," Jim says. "We expect it, even in the troubles of the city."

Appendix
The Ten Commandments
of the Street

In Jim's Own Words

There are rules and then there are rules. The I-don't-know-you rule of the street achieves no lasting good. It's more of an excuse than a rule. I get to deck you if I know you, but if I don't, then I get to steal from you. Boy, that makes sense.

If that rule seems convoluted, don't give up. There are other, time-proven rules that the people who run Neighborhood Fellowship know all about. In this appendix, Jim takes a look at the Ten Commandments as they apply to urban and suburban cultures.

Rule No. 1. Thou shalt have no other gods before me.

Believe it or not, there are gods that prevent suburban people from coming to the city. Everybody does not have to come downtown. But everyone has a responsibility to care for the needy. The church has an overwhelming biblical mandate from God that we should care for the needy.

Here are the gods that people put first:

No. 1. Safety: We hear that from almost everyone. They express that while locking up the SUV, when coming downtown in a smaller car would have been better. There's an aversion to risk that leads, then, to the aversion to go into desperate, crime-infested communities.

The antidote is faith and wisdom. Wisdom would be listening to the voice that says, "Don't go downtown in your new SUV."

No. 2. My children, my children: People say this all the time as a reason not to come and interact. They don't want their children at risk of foul language, bad behavior, parasites and crime. They will not risk them. I'm not suggesting that putting children in harm's way is God's plan. I'm saying that not considering how to overcome the risk makes your children more important than God's command.

No. 3. Pride: There's pride of place, pride of appearance, and pride of relationship. What will people think of me if I associate with the lowly? But it's a command of God to associate with the lowly.

No. 4. General selfishness: People think, *Someone else's need is not my issue.* We often hear from Christians that a need does not equal a call from God. That's a wrong attitude. But if I love them as I do myself, it is a call from God. Of course, you have to distinguish what's a need and what's a want.

There are plenty of gods that exist in the inner city, too. Here are some of them.

No. 1. Entitlement: This is probably the major god. A sub-category is comfort. The reasoning is, we will comfort ourselves with anything and everything because we've suffered too long. I'm an American and I'm poor, so I deserve to have what I want. That's why I steal. I'm entitled to get drunk because it makes me feel better. This leads to all sorts of things, like theft, laziness, and slothfulness.

No. 2. Pride: This is the attitude that nobody can tell me what to do. If there is no father figure at all, what authority is there? If you're not afraid of your father, you're not afraid of the police. If you're not afraid of the police, you're not afraid to commit crimes. You're not afraid of death. So, pride is played out in many ways: pride of place among the affluent; pride of personal control among the poor.

No. 3. Relationship: It becomes your god because it's the only resource you have. You hold on, no matter what it costs you. The affluent can discard relationships if what they are after is things. But if you can't get things, relationship becomes your god. You become part of a group, like the Outlaws gang. Loyalty is how you're known. Putting your trust in the group and its relationships takes the place of God. You trust a bad boyfriend or a lying brother, all for the relationship.

Rule No. 2: You shall make no graven images.

There's a saying, "Jesus wouldn't be welcome in my church because He wouldn't be allowed to bleed on the carpet."

This goes along with graven images. The church building itself, with all of its finery, can be a graven image.

Then, there are the images inside. While it is not inherently wrong to show an image that represents Christ, the picture or engraving is but a limited attempt to show who God is—without the depth, breadth, and reality of the living God. We just say we need to trust Christ and not be limited to any particular view of Him. Your view should be ever-growing and ever-informed.

Now look at what happens in the city. A picture of Christ

as white, particularly effeminate, and exclusively and always gentle can be hoisted up as the singular representation of who God is. Churches are guilty of embracing the picture of Christ and not the actual Christ and His commandments.

In the city, the limited representations of God offered to people with a limited vocabulary or limited life experience and limited education can then limit their ability to have an expanding view of God. They often come with a particularly limited view, and we have to expand it. They've watched television, they've seen images of "only gentle Jesus." Well, the Bible says to fear falling into the hands of an angry God.

Some graven images are larger than the culture. Graven images are rooted in an absolute self-centeredness. It's imagining us as the center of all things. God must be like us.

Another aspect is, the church can unintentionally communicate with its pristine buildings that a relationship with God is unattainable. I couldn't keep my house as clean as that stained glass. The beauty of church buildings can be off-putting to people who live in poverty. Images of Christ don't show him with dirty hands or messy hair. Vice-versa, old, dirty buildings can be off-putting to people who live in wealth.

Rule No. 3: You shall not take the name of the Lord your God in vain.

This verse is about how people use the name of God. The way it applies is, every drug dealer, prostitute, and thief in jail, they're all "Christians." They state with their mouths that they belong to God. They say they love Jesus. But there's no other evidence that they do belong to Him. Those who do not belong to Him but say they do use His name in vain.

The command includes cursing, but that's hardly the way that most people sin against this command. The sin is misrepresenting the name of the Lord. They use His name but say and act as if He has no effect on their lives. It's the hypocrite's greatest sin.

In poverty, breaking this command by cursing is evident because it's so carnal, fleshly and clear. In affluence, it can be cursing, but much more regularly people say they love the Lord but don't love the people He's chosen. They won't give them their time. They won't do as He commands, and that is to help the poor, to help people with overwhelming problems, or to help children. People say they love God but are often too busy with soccer and other activities to bring their children to church. That's the hardest one to give an absolute statement about. It's more ethereal. When are you using His name in vain?

The verse says He will not hold anyone guiltless who misuses His name. The guilt of the Pharisees is, today, on people who talk about their love of God and then don't act like Christians. That is misrepresenting Him and themselves.

If God is standing as invisible, the thing we can corrupt is his reputation. We can by our actions abuse his reputation. This, not his title as God, is what he is holding dear.

Rule No. 4. Remember the Sabbath, to keep it holy.

This command can be explained more technically. The apostles changed everything by saying the Lord's Day is when we worship. So it gets changed from Saturday, day of rest, to Sunday, the day we remember the Lord. It's not that the Sabbath got changed to Sunday, it's that Jesus is our Sabbath rest. We need to rest from our sin, our work. God is the supplier of our rest.

Keeping the Sabbath brings healing. Man is not made

for Sabbath, but the Sabbath for mankind. Those who neglect rest do it at their own peril. The Sabbath is for doing good on the day itself. But ultimate rest comes only in knowing Jesus Christ. Knowing Him brings rest from the pain we bear.

Viewing Sunday as the Sabbath, and not as the Lord's Day, is a misconception. Those locked into that view are shocked at how the world turns Sunday into football, and they are unforgiving of people who can't get to church in the morning because of their lot in life.

We never have had our services in the morning on Sundays. Scripture tells us to "Be all things to all men that you might win some." For slaves, the only time they could hold church services was often at night because they were up at dawn and working in the fields all day. We have applied that to Neighborhood Fellowship, where people are working the only jobs they can get, or have worked the late shift and are asleep. We have adapted to the culture. We have an afternoon service followed by a meal.

Sadly, though, the Lord's Day has become time to play, not to pray in America. The desire for external personal peace and affluence described by theologian Francis Schaeffer is desired more than the internal peace and rest of God—the Sabbath rest.

Rule No. 5: Honor your parents, that it may go well with you.

When Neighborhood Fellowship was starting, we were rehabbing this house so we could live there, the church could meet there, and we could make a difference. My parents divorced at that time, so I inherited my mother.

In the divorce process, I talked to my dad about divorce; I told him this is not what Christians do. He took out a restraining order against me, wanting to take me to court.

The judge threw it out, but I had told lawyers I'd gladly be restrained from further conversations.

My father disowned me and my siblings because of this confrontation. This was a legal disowning. There's an awful hole in my life. Right here on Kessler Boulevard lives this man I haven't seen in 14 years. I saw him mowing the yard, once, after 10 years.

Mother was going to come live with us, and then her own mother needed her. So I inherited both my grandmother and mother. Grandma eventually died, and Mom went to live with her father, until he died. Now she's living in his house until she gets evicted, unless she declares squatters' rights. Then she'll come back to live with us. She is a patient, kind, gentle woman, committed to family.

But Mother is a big pack rat. This causes great tension. I look at her and say, "I love you, but I hate your stuff." We have figured out how to relate to each other. In the end, my father got the family's power and wealth, but my mother got the relationship.

But this command is God's protection for society, whether the parents deserve it or not. It is the provision for us in our old age, it is the building block for world systems, that people care for and honor their parents.

Down here, you often have to honor a father you don't even know. Sometimes, you get to choose, like Jacob and Michelle. Debbie is going to become their mother. They can honor their birth mother, but they also have Debbie to honor.

The opposite of honoring your parents is dishonoring and disrespecting them. In wealthy situations, some may put them away once they become inconvenient. In urban areas, children take advantage of the widow or widower's social security but neglect the parent. They become predators. This is the destruction of society.

The irony of it all is that the younger generations are watching. The honor or dishonor that people deal out to their elderly will become their own lot later on. People who dishonor their own parents will, in turn, find themselves neglected later on. But those who honor their elderly parents are more likely to be treated well by their own children.

I have lost two things in life: I have lost access to my dad. This is irretrievable. It's one of the most painful parts of my life. Blessed are those who mourn. They will be comforted. Most of us at Neighborhood Fellowship know what it is like to be fatherless.

Second, my family was tied to the land. We worked it. It was part of who I am. And so my great love for buildings, institutions, and property is tied to that. I lost my connection to the land, the history. I am bereft of that. I lost any inheritance when my father disowned me. Now I have to figure out how to have something to leave to my children.

It's painful to follow God, but it's worth it.

Rule No. 6: You shall not murder.

I know some murderers. Overall, I'm against murder. That's my official position.

Seriously, the book of Matthew states that hatred is the sin of murder, and 1 John calls Satan "a liar and a murderer from the beginning." He causes us to murder in different forms.

Murder is played out in both cultures. In the suburban culture, it is more common in the area of abortion, which is killing for economic benefit or social standing. People think, *I can't continue in this community in the manner I'm accustomed to if I continue the pregnancy.*

The Life Center on the east side has many clients coming from a specific church. While some keep their babies or put them up for adoption, others have abortions. Has God's demand for purity become a demand for hypocrisy—it's better to cover up the sin than bear the shame?

It's the same in the inner city: I have to murder someone because if I don't, it will affect my social standing. Someone is disrespecting me, and I can't let that pass. I can't show my face if I continue to be disrespected. They also murder for economic gain, which might mean money or things.

In both cultures, the theme is respect.

Jesus also defines murder as hating your brother. He defines hatred as lack of love. It is played out physically in the city: I hate you, so I will kill you. Abandonment is the act of hatred, and it has generational effects. In a sense, you murder those you abandon, particularly if you leave them in anger. This is why Jesus talks about hate being the same as murder. The saying, "You are dead to me," happens every day when people just leave. In a sense, they kill those people they won't relate to anymore.

A man or woman who abandons the family to take on another relationship in every way has murdered that family. If you are willing to hate someone even though you have vowed to love him or her the rest of your life, then you are killing him or her.

Rule No. 7: You shall not commit adultery

This morning I was in a meeting with Friends of the 'Hood at the Cracker Barrel. On my way home, I saw Phil's car going really slowly south down Dearborn, a place it shouldn't be, so I started to follow him. I didn't recognize any of the people in the backseat, so I thought I must have the wrong car. I turned around and went back to Neighborhood Fellowship.

It turned out it was indeed Phil (Debbie's father and elder at Neighborhood Fellowship) and Kristy Alsmeyer in the van. Kristy explained there was a woman who asked Phil if he'd give her a ride the rest of the way home, about a half mile. She was worn out and frozen.

Phil then asked Kristy to come along. The lady gave them a hard luck story on the way home. She was separated (not divorced) from her husband, and oh, it had been so difficult. Oh, and her boyfriend was cheating on her, too.

When Phil said that, I just roared. I told Deb the story, and she roared. This is my "Thou shalt not commit adultery" story.

The very fiber of our communities is torn to bits by adultery. We individually look at this type of sin and say, "Well, we survived that." We don't look at the collective result of sin on the larger community. If you're only worried about the first domino hitting the second, you've got a problem, especially if there are hundreds of dominoes out there. Adultery has a ripple effect that doesn't end until someone says, "This will stop here." There will be degeneration into debauchery and hopelessness.

Only the church will say that about adultery and its fallout. It has to. People are wise enough at some point to mourn the blessings they have lost. They will cry out to God. That is the beginning of wisdom.

8. You shall not steal.

Jim tells of a neighbor who goes to work five days a week and while he's gone, he gets robbed. They come in and take his TV and his food.

It probably doesn't help that he keeps hanging around prostitutes. Their boyfriends come over and do the looting.

Stealing is the end result of coveting. James tells us that there is a progression to sin.

We once walked up on a man slamming a rock through a car window. There were eight of us—the whole family. The strange thing is, we thought nothing of it. We cannot walk two blocks without something incredible happening. We watched as a Hispanic man came running out of a nearby house yelling, "That's my car!" The Hispanic man hauled the African American from his car and called 911, but he gave the wrong street name. I decided to call 911 myself and give the correct street. Deb took the kids around the corner. So now, I'm enmeshed. I can see a fight is about to ensue. Abigail is excited we are doing something good, standing in defense of this Hispanic man, and I take a picture with my cell phone. The black man runs off. The police arrive and yell at the Hispanic man to get his hands out of his pockets, but he doesn't understand. The officer yells again, and he still doesn't understand, so they start to frisk the guy. He's the victim. He's telling police, "You're too late, you're too late." I explain it all to the officer, in English.

But this thief robbed our family of time. He robbed the peace of my community. He robbed the victim of his dignity because he was treated like a criminal when he wasn't. He robbed me of a sense of being able to sort things out. I felt pretty stupid. If I had assessed the situation quicker, I could have grabbed the guy. Now this fellow (the car thief) is looking for us, and we're watching out for him.

The thief gave me something, too. Theft gives you a real sense of the depravity of man, so you have a clear understanding of sin and the evilness of it.

In the suburbs you have theft, but you don't see it.

We also live in a cult of capitalism: I get mine, but I'm not worried about the worker who produced what I have.

Eminent domain is another way of stealing. We experienced this when they tried to steal our building (see chapter 3).

9. You shall not bear false witness against your neighbor.

Satan is a liar, the father of lies. When you bear false witness, you have engaged in the greatest treason there is, because that is what the other side does. We are commanded to speak the truth in love.

Lies are told with words, and lies are told with actions. If you treat a person with disrespect, you are saying to him, "You are of no value," and that is a lie. Everyone has value. This tends to be the attitude toward the poor—being dismissive, staying away, talking down to them without knowing them.

Sometimes a lie is a veneer of politeness where the truth goes unspoken. You learn to lie, but in polite ways. (You don't think a certain couple should get married, but instead of speaking the truth in love, you just don't attend the wedding.) You don't speak up when a lie is being told.

The poor people's lies are usually to get themselves out of trouble. The truth is, "I'm a thief, and I will steal from you." Their lies, then, are a cover for evil actions: "I didn't mean to," or "I didn't do that." Pathological liars live here. There are lies to avoid immediate pain. For instance, a mother deserts her children but says she is going on a vacation. It is their language because they are lost.

10. You shall not covet.

Some people covet their own stuff and money. Many people want to solve poverty, while others look the other way. The Lord says, "The poor you will always have with you, so be generous." But many people don't hear that part about being generous. They hear, "The poor you will always have with you, so you don't need to do anything." If you are commanded to be generous and you are not, it's because you are greedy and greed is just another form of covetousness.

Covetousness is a way to keep what you have gathered together. You say to yourself, "Now that I figured out how to get it, I need to figure out how to keep it."

Scripture tells us, "Let him who steals steal no longer, but work with his hands so he can share with others." What we have, God gives us to share with others.

At the same time, when people begin to think other people's money or stuff is the answer to their problems, this is covetousness. This takes God out of the equation. Remember that God is the provider, not other people.

God says to Abraham, "I'm going to bless you. I will be your great reward." If we are satisfied with the creator and not the stuff He's created, then things will go well. God is our reward and blessing. This is the best possession on earth, whether you are poor or rich.

Poor people are covetous in ways you cannot imagine. There is the hoarder who hoards, to his great destruction. Hoarding is a response to poverty. People hoard because they think, *I might need that. I need to take care of myself.* This is a matter of the heart, of not trusting God.

Here's a new command: **Love your neighbor as yourself!**